BEYOND THE METROPOLIS: VILLAGES IN HONG KONG

COMPILED TO MARK THE 35TH ANNIVERSARY OF THE FOUNDING OF
THE HONG KONG BRANCH OF THE ROYAL ASIATIC SOCIETY

1995

BEYOND THE METROPOLIS: VILLAGES IN HONG KONG

EDITORS:

P.H. HASE

ELIZABETH SINN

GRAPHICS ADVISER:

JOHN LAMBON

CONTRIBUTORS:

PHOTOGRAPHY

RICHARD ABRAHALL, ARPS

KIM APLIN, ARPS

ANDY DOMERACKI

TONY HEDLEY

JOHN LAMBON

JANET STOTT, ARPS

RICHARD STOTT, LRPS

TEXT

RICHARD GEE

PATRICK HASE

JAMES W. HAYES

ROSEMARY LEE

DAVID LUNG

ELIZABETH SINN

JOSEPH TING

DAN D. WATERS

RICHARD WEBB

BEYOND THE METROPOLIS: VILLAGES IN HONG KONG

JOINT PUBLISHING (H.K.) COMPANY LIMITED

BEYOND THE METROPOLIS: VILLAGES IN HONG KONG

THE ROYAL ASIATIC SOCIETY, HONG KONG BRANCH

PUBLISHING EDITOR: CHENG TAK WAH

DESIGNER: LUK CHI CHEONG

Published by

JOINT PUBLISHING (H.K.) CO., LTD.
9 Queen Victoria Street, Hong Kong

FIRST PUBLISHED IN DECEMBER 1995

SECOND IMPRESSION APRIL 2000

Colour separation by

FINE ARTS REPRO HOUSE CO., LTD.
Kin Teck Industrial Building, 26 Wong Chuk Hang Road, Hong Kong

Printed in Hong Kong by

C&C OFFSET PRINTING CO., LTD.
36 Ting Lai Road, Tai Po, N.T., Hong Kong

ISBN 962-04-1298-2

VILLAGES: INTRODUCTION

ELIZABETH SINN

It would be difficult to conceive of a more appropriate way to celebrate the Royal Asiatic Society, Hong Kong Branch's 35th Anniversary than with a book on Hong Kong's villages.

Since the Hong Kong Branch of the Royal Asiatic Society was re-established in 1959, the New Territories, with its largely rural communities, has been an area of immense interest. While lectures on scientific and cultural topics of East Asia have been regularly arranged in keeping with the Society's traditional objective of introducing Asia to the world at large, 'expeditions' it organized were inevitably focused on places of historical and archaeological interests inside Hong Kong. And, therefore, inevitably, on the villages of the New Territories.

One highlight of the Society's activities in its early years was a weekend symposium in May 1964 entitled 'Aspects of Social Organization in the New Territories'. It comprised one full day of lectures and another of conducted visits to villages in five different districts. The proceedings, with seven articles covering various aspects of village life, including clan organization, family life, ancestor worship and

so forth, and brief reports on each of the villages visited, were published and subsequently went into a second printing. This publication, a pioneer effort in this area of scholarship, remains a basic reference.

The Society, through publishing articles and organizing tours to the New Territories for three and a half decades, has played, and continues to play, a leading role in drawing the attention both of scholars and the informed general public to the historical and cultural value of that area. Until the 1950s, few Chinese scholars had done empirical research on the New Territories, possibly because of its peripheral cultural position in 'Mainstream China', i.e. China of the 'Great Tradition'. Both in geographical and cultural terms, the New Territories, with its predominantly non-gentry population, is about as far away as one could get from Beijing, the Yellow River or Yangzi River basins, the centres of 'Chinese Culture', and therefore, it was deemed unworthy of scholarly attention by traditional scholars. And yet, ironically, as China battled to erase its feudal past after 1949, it is Hong Kong (and Taiwan, though in a different way), which has become the repository

of Chinese traditions — in Hong Kong, in part at least because it has been a British colony.

In the New Territories, in particular, it may be claimed that 'rural China' has continued unchanged (or at least, changing only gradually) for centuries. Not surprisingly, anthropologists and sociologists from the West wanting to study 'Chinese society', but denied the opportunity to conduct fieldwork in the People's Republic of China, came, from the 1950s, to the New Territories, to look to this outpost of the Chinese Empire for data and inspiration.

A lot of water has gone under the bridge since the Symposium on the New Territories 30 years ago. Many of the contributors to that Symposium, then budding scholars, including Hugh Baker and James Hayes, have gone on to become world-renowned authorities. Other scholars, likewise closely connected with the Society but too young to have taken part in that event, have since then propelled research in this area in new directions, uncovered new information, gained new insights. It is time for a general re-examination.

More importantly, the New Territories itself

has undergone sea-changes. Urban and industrial developments have caught up with the villages. Following the drive in the 1970s to redistribute Hong Kong's population into the countryside, the New Territories population has jumped from just under 700,000 in 1971 to about 2.37 million in 1991, thus severely reducing the proportion of indigenous villagers, (estimated in 1986 at roughly 460,000 with 260,000 living abroad) within New Territories society. Obviously, this emigration of over half of the indigenous villagers, and the inflow of non-indigenous people has had devastating effects on indigenous New Territories villages. Villages, once nestled in green valleys, now linger a little forlornly, in the shadow of high-rise apartment buildings, if they are not abandoned altogether in ruins; the countless television cables and satellite dishes and containers stacked high in yards which had once been fish ponds or paddy and vegetable fields, have at the same time damaged their fung shui. The villages, it appears, are fighting a rearguard battle against the advent of the metropolis.

And yet, if we look beyond the television cables, and the highways and shopping malls, we may still find vestiges of the village tradition. For many of the villagers, whether working in fields, factories or offices, the emotional ties with the land, the home of their ancestors for ten, twenty, or thirty generations, remain unchanged. The sense of being part of a long tradition and the desire to perpetuate it, too, remains unchanged. These poignant sentiments colour much of their outlook on the world, and outsiders may begin to grasp this deep-rooted mentality only if they shed their customary cynicism, and look and listen with sensitivity. Then they may find that, in face of the advent of the metropolis, the villages are demonstrating the same resilience that has enabled them to survive for a millennium.

This book of photographs attempts to capture New Territories villages as they were in 1993/94. As most of the studies of villages to date have been textual, this album represents a breakthrough in the documentation and presentation of the subject. More importantly, the excellent photography has made the album a work of rare beauty.

In terms of content, this book is divided into two parts: one on general themes, the other on individual villages and districts. The essays cover the political, economic, social and cultural dimensions of village life, as it was, and as it is. The different training and backgrounds of the authors add diversity to the topics, and highlight the multifacetedness and complexity of that life.

In their own rights, the essays are a worthwhile collection of research findings, but here they serve the additional purpose of helping readers interpret the photographs with greater understanding, and so of enhancing their enjoyment.

Many people have worked long and hard to make this book possible. The Council wishes to thank the f8 photographers and all the authors for their invaluable contribution, and members of the 35th Anniversary Book Project Committee for their time and ideas.

The Council is also indebted to Jebsen & Co. Ltd. for its generous donation of Ilford film and paper.

Dr. Elizabeth Sinn is the Vice-President of the RAS and Chairman of the Historical Buildings Committee of the Antiquities Advisory Board. She has published widely on the history of Modern China and Hong Kong , in both English and Chinese. Her latest book is *Society and Culture in Hong Kong*.

CONTENTS

LOCATION MAP

The Satellite Image of Hong Kong was reproduced with the permission of Geocarto International Centre
© 1992 RSGS China and GIC Hong Kong

● PLACES MENTIONED
■ PHOTOGRAPHS

CHAPTER ONE

THE TRADITIONAL BACKGROUND:
HONG KONG VILLAGES IN THE 1950S

THE TRADITIONAL BACKGROUND:

HONG KONG VILLAGES IN THE 1950S

JAMES W. HAYES

INTRODUCTION

The twenty years from the 1950s to the 1970s saw the end of rice farming over most of the New Territories. With the ending of rice farming came a weakening of the social structure built around it. The same twenty years also saw the disappearance of most village artisan skills, as city products swept the rural markets. The younger people began to see no hope in life in their ancestral villages, and began to move out, to the city or overseas, in search of work and a better life. By the 1970s many old settlements had become depopulated. These trends have intensified over the last twenty years. In the 1990s, New Territories and New Territories village life, are merely tattered remnants of the old vibrant and long established local culture. What was life like in the villages in the mid-1950s, when the traditional way of life was still largely untouched? During this mid-1950s period, as District Officer in the old Southern District (the present Sai Kung and Islands Districts), I visited some 180 settlements, and made notes on all of them.Following a year's language study, District Officer, South, was my first post in the Hong Kong Civil Service, and since I had no previous background or experience, I felt I had to get to grips with the District and its people. Familiarization visits were thus high on the agenda, often travelling by boat but ultimately on foot, in the many areas where there were as yet no roads. As I visited each settlement, I walked round it with the elders, and then sat down with them to take down details of each community and discuss

any problems. These jottings have remained in two small notebooks since that time, only in part transcribed.

The contents of this chapter are mostly verbatim transcriptions form these notes. Clarificatory material has been added in square brackets. Their interest lies in the picture they present of an essentially rural and conservative society; one which no longer exists in the completely altered conditions of modern Hong Kong.

SOME VILLAGE COMMUNITIES AND THE RURAL ECONOMY

1.Wong Chuk Shan, Sai Kung

There are a reported 133 persons in the village. There are 25 families of Chung and only one of Sham. Curiously enough, despite the great disparity in their numbers the forbears of both families came together and at the same time, nine generations ago, from Changle District, Eastern Guangdong. All are Hakkas. There are 27 children over the age of 6, and all go to school. The village school holds 27 pupils, with 19 from Wong Chuk Shan, plus 4 more from Mau Ping, another hill village but located within Taipo District.

The villagers [mainly the women] farm 150 tau chung of padi and about 10 of vegetable land. [The "tau chung" was a local measure of the amount of land that could be planted with a bushel of rice seed as measured by a "tau container" made of wood. There were usually about six tau chung to the acre.] They have 40

cows and 3 sows. There is no forestry lot or orchard, just a few tangerine trees, and the Village Representative [also known as the village headman] said they would like to apply for a "Kadoorie Orchard" from the Kadoorie Agricultural Aid Association.

Two men are in Borneo, and 4 are working in Hong Kong or Kowloon. However, apart from farming, the main occupation of the men seems to be the construction business. Several employ their own relatives and other male villagers from the Sai Kung area, and travel round the New Territories building houses. [This was a traditional rural artisan's trade, often concentrated in several villages in a District, as here: usually mountainside villages such as Wong Chuk Shan supplemented their inadequate rice harvests by operating a peripatetic artisan's trade in the slack time between harvests.]

They have proposed to install a better water supply, to include two storage tanks and requiring 900 feet of piping to bring water from a suitable intake. They applied for 500 bags last year from our Local Public Works vote. [Public funds designed to assist rural communities to undertake self-help improvements. Trained District Office staff also provided technical advice.] They got 200 bags then and would like the rest any time. Our Assistant Inspector of Works will look into it. Since they are building contractors they should have no difficulty doing a satisfactory job.

[The inhabitants of Wong Chuk Shan moved away from the village, and it became completely abandoned in the 1970s. The

For 250 years, Cheung Uk has stood at the foot of its fung shui hill looking out over its fields. The oldest houses lie closest to the wood and with each succeeding generation, rows of houses have been added to the front to form the close packed mass of brick walls, tiled roofs and stone-flagged lanes which we see today.

Blue brick fired in local kilns form the outside walls of traditional
village houses. They are usually thickly plastered to keep out the rain.
Any windows are small and barred against intruders.

death-knell of the village was the switch to concrete rather than the traditional stone and brick houses, rendering the village's artisan skills no longer wanted.]

2. Ngong Wo, Sai Kung

An upland village, very pleasant and with splendid views. The village representative told us there were 74 persons, all Laus in some 19 households, living here. They have been here for over a hundred years, coming from northeastern Guangdong. Another 7 Lau families from this place are now living at Tai Wan village, and 3 more in Sai Kung Market. There are another 20 persons living in Wong Chuk Wan, down below, an offshoot from the main settlement, established for four generations and therefore nearly as old as Ngong Wo itself. Among those families in residence at Ngong Wo, none of the men work outside, save for one in England. Ten children are in the 6-16 age group, but as there is no school they go elsewhere to study.

The families at Ngong Wo are farming 40-50 tau chung, and another 4-5 tau chung of vegetable land. They have enough rice, with exchange, to give them a four to five months' supply. [It was then the practice for villagers to take their own, better quality, unhusked rice to a miller, who would give them in return the same weight in husked imported rice.] The Wong Chuk Wan families are worse off, even with exchange having only enough for 3 months, and having to buy for the rest of the year. [These low figures were not unusual, as the 90 persons at nearby Shan Liu also had only a three months' supply.] There are 25 brown cows, 4 cows and 25 porkers at Ngong Wo. They have sufficient potable water, but not enough for irrigation needs. There is a fish pond in front of the houses, and they want 160 bags of cement to make some repairs.

The villagers have just finished the lower part of an intended "road" leading from behind Wong Chuk Wan and up to the village, probably along the line of the previous path. It had taken them 2 months, and they said they had spent $700 on food. In answer to my question how they had financed this, they said they had sold trees. This would explain the tremendous amount of cut wood stacked round the houses. They explained that wood cutting was their major activity in winter, and complained about the Port Shelter Firing Range. This took in the hill land above the village, and prior to its establishment, they had been used to cutting firewood there 7 days a week in the wintertime. Nowadays, it was closed to them for 4 days a week. Moreover, trees were destroyed by firing the larger guns so that they had less wood to sell. They mentioned the magic word "compensation", but did not pursue it.

[Ngong Wo also became totally abandoned by the 1970s, in this case the abandonment was assisted by the switch from burning firewood to using kerosene and LPG (liquified petroleum gas in cylinders) for cooking. As the firewood market disappeared, Ngong Wo became unviable as a village.]

3. The "Six Villages", Sai Kung

[Some of my visits were to the "Six Villages", a group of settlements centred on Pak Tam Chung, beyond the then end of the Sai Kung Road.] Pak Tam Chung is more of a central place, giving access to (and from) the sea at a nearby landing place. There are some houses and shops, and a newly-built school whose construction and running expenses were subsidized by Government. The school serves all the nearby villages, but not all the children of school age in the villages attend.

The head man made a request for cement and other Local Public Works materials in the coming August to build a badly-needed bridge, and then spoke of a protective wall being needed at the creek. Salt water had flooded the fields and last year "relief rice" had been given for 15 tau chung. ["Relief rice" was given to help out by the Districe Office in time of difficulty or to provide food when villagers were working on local public works. It was described to me as being "no better than sweepings" at one or two villages.] The request had been made two years before and the Irrigation Engineer had inspected the site, but nothing had been done.

From discussing the relief rice, we got onto selling prices of local products. Unhusked rice was currently worth $39 per picul. This was cheap, as it was usually $42-43. Dry firewood was being sold in Sai Kung for $3.50 a picul, but the other local fuel, dried grass, was not selling, as no one would take it, [because of the switch to kerosene and LPG.] Pigs sold for $140 last year, and were now $200. Local tangerines were selling for $120 a picul this years; [this was a winter, and especially lunar new year, crop.]

These items are taken to Sai Kung Market by the "Six Villages" Pig Raising Cooperative's own cargo junk. The charge is 20 cents a picul. The Committee had purchased and now ran this boat. It had cost $2000, and they had paid $1000 for another, smaller one. Five villagers were hired to run the two boats, and each man was paid $90 monthly. The boats needed to make $5 a day to meet their running expenses, roughly half this amount each. However, they were not now even getting $2 each, as only about 5 or 6 persons were travelling daily to Sai Kung, paying 30 cents each way, and extra for whatever produce they took with them. The provision of such boats was stated to be "a traditional rural practice" in the area - meaning that it was a necessity. The Chairman of the Committee comes from Wong Yi Chau. In addition to the two boats run by the Committee from Pak Tam Chung, the Chairman himself also runs another boat from Wong Yi Chau to Sai Kung. This is a 20 foot sailing sampan, with no motor, carrying between 10-20 persons and charging 30 cents one way, and 10 cents for a basket of rice or vegetables.

Wong Yi Chau is a big village, as local settlements go, with two subsidiary hamlets. The Chairman reported 135 inhabitants. They farmed around 150 tau chung of padi fields, and exchanged the unhusked rice for poorer quality rice at shops in Sai Kung Market, but even so, received only enough for half the year's needs, and had to buy the rest. They had about 20 brown cattle. Their livelihood also came from pig rearing and selling firewood. There were currently 200 pigs in the village of which 15 were sows. Pigs fetched $150-160 a picul. Some remittances came from 5 men working abroad, all employed in Chinese restaurants in Liverpool. Another man worked in Hong Kong with the tram company, but there was none working in Sai Kung or Kowloon. Some of the villagers are Christians. There is a Protestant chapel in the village, said to be already 60 years old. A pastor came to hold services each Sunday. Some other village people go to the Catholic Church at Pak Tam Chung.

The villagers suffer from insufficient drinking water in the dry season, and wish to have cement and other materials to build a well. They had also applied for cement to build an irrigation dam four months ago.

[Pig raising was obviously a chancy business in the 1950s.] The people at Yau Yue Wan on Junk Bay rear pigs on a large scale, but said they had lost a lot of money when 50-60 pigs died just before the Chinese New Year. The disease was reported to the Government Agricultural Station at Sai Kung. Some couldn't repay their loans, and others only managed to repay half, so were unable to get any more. They used to have 600 pigs, but were now down to about 100. They did not know the name of the disease.

[The Six Villages area lost most of its population in the 1960s, as better located villages with road access could supply pigs cheaper than the Six Villages, dependent on ferries. However, the extension of the Sai Kung Road to Pak Tam Chung allowed villagers in the villages along the new road to work in the city, and these villages remain inhabited, although those villages well off the new road, including Wong Yi Chau, were mostly abandoned in the 1970s. Yau Yue Wan was recently resited because of the Junk Bay New Town Development.]

SOME OF THE REALTIES OF VILLAGE LIFE

One of my notebooks contains an entry about a dispute between two of the larger Sai Kung villages over a grave, in which the aggrieved parties "wanted the other side to pay for 10,000 strings of firecrackers to be discharged at their ancestral hall in a show of public atonement."

This is a reminder that village people could be quite quarrelsome in those days. Their communities were usually old, lives could be complicated by long-standing grudges and animosities, and it was fortunate for Government that the Village Representatives and elders could usually take care of such matters. "The Police and the DO being far away" - as one of my informants put it - the burden of settling disputes fell mainly on the Village Representatives. I have come across enough evidence to show that the number of such cases was not small. A 49 year old Village Representative made a sworn statement in 1950, in which he said he had settled around 500 disputes during his time in the post. Another of my elderly village friends, a former

Chairman of the Tsing Yi Rural Committee, has estimated that, when Village Representative, he used to have to settle around 40-50 cases a year in the late 1940s and '50s. These had comprised petty quarrels and assaults, including marital affairs, trespass by cows, damage to crops, boundary disputes and the like. In a case of this sort, another Village Representative from Tsing Yi recalled how he had settled a dispute in which a woman whose three big longan trees had been chopped down by an infuriated relative over some petty issue, now forgotten, had been pacified by his giving her some money.

The Village Representatives were the village managers, but the post was not a bed of roses. If the Village Representative had to settle a dispute, then he faced the sensitive task of adjudicating between fellow-clansmen, and fellow-villagers. The village was then still a very close knit community, with many internal ties through marriage going back over generations. A friend from my District Officer, South, days has explained how there was a set of constraints on the headman's action in most ordinary rural and family concerns. They included the constraint of friendship: the constraint of neighbourliness: and the constraint of belonging to the same clan: and all concerned had to continue living together in the same place after the intervention.

Against these disadvantages, he said, some factors operated in the Village Representatives' favour. The old way of life, with its constant anxieties about the vagaries of the weather and the ever-present threat of typhoon damage to houses, field crops and irrigation systems, put a premium on co-operation and solidarity. Villagers had to cultivate those virtues, or else find themselves literally helpless in an emergency. In any disagreement between people, the Village Representatives and elders would act as middlemen and help resolve the

SHA LO TUNG JOHN LAMBON

The roofs of village houses are made up of two interlocking layers of curved tiles.
The air trapped between the tiles kept the roof cool and provided guttering for rain water.

23

problem, as it was in everybody's interest to maintain unity. In those days, people took their problems to the headmen: they themselves did not go looking for work. Moreover, the headmen still had considerable authority, especially if they were capable managers and knew how to handle people, and they were greatly helped by the continuing strength of traditional ethics among the villagers. People had a good idea of what was going on, and under the old-fashioned education which most of the men had received and the traditional upbringing that all had received, had a keenly developed sense of what was right or wrong. Thus, if a Village Representative took the lead in condemning someone's actions and was correct in his assessment, he was likely to get support from the majority, who might have hesitated to speak out as individuals. These were the bases of village management at that time.

In those days, too, staff of government departments and the New Territories and Marine Police were glad to work in with the village leaders. It made their own job easier, and was mutually supportive. If petty matters were referred back to the Village Representatives and elders to deal with, village authority was also sustained.

EDUCATION:
GIRLS STILL DISADVANTAGED

On my visits to the villages, I soon encountered the traditional discrimination against female schooling. Some twelve years after the War, it was still very much in evidence; for although a good many boys were not going to school, far more girls were not getting any education. The notebooks are revealing not just for the numbers recorded, but for attitudes too. At Shan Shek Wan on South Lantau, children not going to school (others did) had included

(in the speaker's words) "some who are too small, a few girls, and some boys who have to look after the cows". In one of the Tung Chung villages in an adjoining area of the island, a place where education and much else was then at a low ebb, I recorded that "only four children of school age are studying, three of them boys and one girl".

In some areas the provision of schooling for either sex was still inadequate. In conversation with the school teacher in the Tai Mong Tsai Valley, it seemed that only 40 children attended school here out of 106 of school age; but the next term would see a start to two sessions per day, with a second teacher. However, the Government's drive to provide subsidized primary schools all over the New Territories would, during the period 1955-1965, provide affordable school places in all but the smallest villages; and even there, a centrally-located school would be provided to serve a group of nearby settlements. Provision of an adequate number of school places would have its biggest effect on the education of girls, who within a few years would no longer suffer from the old discrimination. Judging by the decided interest shown by some mothers in Ta Ho Tun near Sai Kung Market in school extension, it was clear to me that though without education themselves, they wanted their daughters to go to school. As a consequence of the abandonment of villages and the increasing availability of larger schools in the New Town, most of these village schools closed down during the 1970s and 1980s, and only a handful still remain in operation. However, there can be no doubt about the enthusiasm shown by villagers to the "new schools" in the 1950s.

THE SHADOW OF THE PAST

In some places, but especially among villages on Lantau Island, I found that the past

lay heavily on the present. There was visual evidence of decline in many villages. Owing to misfortune, some villages had been hard hit during the Japanese Occupation; but for many settlements the war years were merely the culmination of bad times that had endured for decades and been characterized by sickness and disease, and by a decline in population and male births. For these phenomena the villagers had no rational explanation, but sought one in the local fung shui that, they presumed, had been altered for the worse and become deadly.

Keung Shan on Lantau, with its Upper and Lower Villages, settled for ten generations, was one of these places. All my informants agreed that the population had greatly decreased. One Village Representative said that before he was born there had been 120 men and boys in his clan, but that there had been many deaths when the Kwun Yam Temple was built (in 1909-10). All believed that its construction had altered the fung shui of the villages. A woman who married out about 1920-21, spoke of small numbers of residents and ruined and unoccupied houses when she was a girl. Her father had had three wives, taken one after the other, owing to deaths. Her own mother, the second, had died when she was very small. Besides the Kwun Yam Temple, another place is credited with having killed off many of the people at Keung Shan. This was "Demons' Pool" a hole or pond dug by farmers from Wang Hang village, closer to Tai O, at a date not now remembered exactly. It had been filled in after being identified as the cause of the deaths. As for the Temple, the other Village Representative said there was nothing the villagers could do about that, as it had been built by a nun who had connections with the Governor of the day: "She had worked at Government House, and the Governor was her godson." Also, this person seems to have been able to command ample funds and support, judging by the couplets in the temple, written by monks and some local gentry and presented at its foundation.

These events - the deaths and reduced numbers, the ruined houses and the general decline in family fortunes - help to explain why there was so much concern at Keung Shan when the Government began to open ground and construct roads and catch waters there in the late 1950s, in connection with the Shek Pik Reservoir project. I had been asked to pay for protective rituals to neutralize the ill effects, and to build a small temple on the side of a catchwater; intended as an upgrading of existing supernatural protection, as there had always been an earthgod shrine at that spot. In 1990, I passed by this temple during a walk through the area with a friend, and found that according to a commemorative tablet, it had been repaired in 1976, with $100 and $50 donations, and now had an image as well as an altar.

VILLAGERS AND PUBLIC WORKS

In other places, it was not the past but present concerns that mattered. In 1959-60 the Sai Kung Road was being extended some five miles along the coast to Tai Mong Tsai, passing through or close to villages on the way. Fields had to be resumed and compensation paid for land and crops. I had problems in getting the road past the small village of Tso Wo Hang, half way along. The Tai Wan people thought the compensation rate was too low, stopped the work, and lined up their women with nightsoil buckets when we went to the village; but it sticks in my mind that none of the inhabitants in the other villages affected by the new road was as temperamental or difficult as the Tso Wo Hang folk.

A note says "The Village Representative asked if the new road could go behind the village, owing to the fact that the villagers had only a little cultivated land." It could not, because of adjoining alignments; but this is interesting, since villagers would usually oppose going behind a village, on fung shui grounds: but here, economic reasons had prevailed. On the other hand, fung shui would soon raise its head during the road works. A brief note mentions "fung shui - confrontation", followed by the query, "work after the crop is cut?" There is another note about cutting stone near Tso Wo Hang Village: the Village Representative was to say when work could begin. It seems that this was a sensitive fung shui spot, where the villagers wanted to do the work themselves. However, as they asked to be paid at the same price as "outside" i.e. Kowloon, where masons got $3 a yard for cutting stone, this rather indicated that they wished to hire out the job, making something for themselves in the process.

In this regard, the Village Representative and his villagers had been quick to realize that they could exert some pressure on the District Office on account of the road works and the need for their cooperation. Another note says: "The Village Representative says he had applied for a piece of Crown land [probably for cultivation] in 1957, but so far has not got it. He also says that 5 villagers would like the District Office to get them employment as earth coolies [with the road contractor], as they can't get the jobs on their own." A request was also made on behalf of a young man who wanted to join the Roads Office. But even when they were offered work as earth coolies by the contractor, the Tso Wo Hang folks were choosy about it. The work was paid at the rate of $3.80 a day for shifting 10 cubic feet [1 cheung] daily. They had not considered this enough and so didn't work. On the other hand, Kowloon people reportedly worked for $3 per day, and normally a contractor would not expect to pay more in the country than in town.

CONCLUSION

Today, visitors to the New Territories villages often find them empty, of half-empty. Most of the adult males are living away. Many of the houses are empty or ruined. The fields are abandoned and waste, or used by outsider vegetable farmers. Visitors notice the beauty of the village setting, nestling below the hills and backed by the dense wall of fung shui trees, but the old, hard life has disappeared. Most of this book celebrates the beauty of the villages, or their deep historical roots. In this short article I have attempted to complete the picture by sketching the realities of life in the villages on the eve of modernisation and the abandonment of traditional village life.

Dr. James W. Hayes, is the immediate past President of the RAS. After several decades in Hong Kong, he has published numerous books and articles on many aspects of its life and history. His latest book is Tsuen Wan, Growth of a New Town and Its People.

SHA LO TUNG, CHEUNG UK   RICHARD ABRAHALL

Couplets, lucky papers and door gods decorate village doors to greet the New Year. Under the eaves those houses which could afford it have bands of painted or stucco decorations. Many houses have added windows in recent years to lighten dark interiors.

HOK TAU WAI RICHARD ABRAHALL

*Solid doors which can be locked at night and when the house is empty, sliding doors which can be closed with the main door open
to allow light and air into the house, and half doors to stop the dogs and pigs from coming into the house: the door of a village
house can be a complex affair.*

Mud bricks dried in the sun are used for walls - like this courtyard wall -which do not carry heavy weight. Blue brick is used for the jambs of the gate, and a timber beam for the head.

SHA LO TUNG, CHEUNG UK   RICHARD ABRAHALL

SHA LO TUNG, CHEUNG UK   RICHARD ABRAHALL

*Many villagers have left their homes to work in the city or overseas. The houses are left barred
and locked. Sooner or later, termites cause the roof to fall in, the rain washes away the mud brick
walls and all that is left are ruins, destined sooner or later to disappear.*

*The older village windows had no glass. During the day, they were closed
with iron bars and at night with stout wooden shutters. Many villages,
like San Uk Tsai, were surrounded with walls. Sometimes the walls have
been removed leaving only a stump on either side of the gate.*

Traditionally, the area near the village was used to store firewood, or straw, and for pasturing cattle. Alas, today it is today it is more likely that it is used for dumping waste.

PAK MONG, NGAU KWU LONG   RICHARD STOTT

NEAR LIN AU   RICHARD ABRAHALL

CHAPTER TWO

THE VILLAGE LANDSCAPE

HOK TAU WAI   RICHARD ABRAHALL

THE VILLAGE LANDSCAPE

RICHARD WEBB

Traditional villages in the New Territories are intimately linked with their surrounding landscapes in ways which may not be immediately apparent to a casual observer.

Typically, a New Territories village nestles at the foot of a slope with ridges of higher ground running down on either side, forming an "armchair" shape. The village is protected at the rear by a woodland with many large and ancient trees. A large banyan tree with a shrine at its foot often protects the entrance to the village. On the ridges beside the village, tangerine and longan trees can often be found, enhancing the embrace the ridges give to the village which lies between them. Usually rather further from the village, and out of sight, are the graves of the ancestors. In front of the village there is normally a wide flat area, now usually concreted, formerly used to dry rice (wo tong), beyond which may be a small pool (ming tong). Crossed by many small streams, the now disused paddy fields stretch out in front of the terraces of houses.

The most important village buildings, especially ancestral halls and temples, share this "armchair" shape. In them, the altars, the heart of the buildings, are protected and embraced by side wings and face into a flat courtyard. Traditional tombs, too, share this general shape. Tombs, ancestral halls, and temples, are all important to a village community. As the village should nestle within the protective embrace of the surrounding hills, so should the buildings at the heart of the community nestle within the protective embrace of man-made walls.

We can see this layout in any typical village landscape in the rural parts of the New Territories not yet disfigured by container depots and car dumps, such as at Lin Au near Tai Po.

This once productive landscape forms a geographical pattern unique to south China, and the key to understanding this pattern is the traditional belief system known as "fung shui". At its most basic, fung shui is the study of the intangible forces inherent in the very fabric of the earth. These forces influence human destiny and well being. Life lived in harmony with these forces is life lived in harmony with the land, and will be a life of peace and prosperity. Life lived in the best possible relationship with these intangible forces of the earth will receive the greatest benefit from the fung shui of the place, and the traditional village landscape in the New Territories is an attempt to ensure this.

The basic idea of fung shui is that some places within the landscape are better for human activities than others. Fung shui assumes that the entire cosmos is made up of the interwoven flow of "yin", the female principle, (inflowing, deep, dark, mysterious and fecund) and "yang", the male principle, (outflowing, vigorous, bright, and life-giving). The contact between yin and yang produces the fundamentals of matter, the five elements of wood, fire, metal, earth and water. In the vortices of the flow of the yin and yang, particles of the elements come together and coalesce, forming the earth and its inhabitants, the stars, and the whole vault of heaven. This, the physical universe, remains in being since it is sustained by the continuing flow of the yin

and yang through it and around it.

Within the world, the yin principle has a natural affinity for valleys, and cool, damp, shady places; in particular areas of flat land at the foot of hills. The yang principle, on the other hand, has a natural affinity for sun-drenched, bare, bright hillslopes.

The inherent forces of the earth flow naturally over the surface of the earth from the yang areas to the yin areas, and then seep back through the hidden underground veins of the earth to the yang areas. These hidden underground "dragon veins" along which the yin forces return to the yang can be likened to the accupuncture meridians in the human body. Deep cuttings into the earth, or deep wells, are, therefore, dangerous as they might damage this vital system.

Fung shui (literally "wind and water") is so named because the yang flows much in the same way as wind; from the mountains, through the valleys to the plains: whereas the yin flows in much the same way as water, gathering in the low ground and seeping away to underground springs and veins.

The forces of fung shui, the flow of yin and yang, are neither good nor bad in themselves, but can be dangerous in some circumstances. The yang force is vigorous, but, in excess, it is violent: it is life-giving, but in excess it can overpower the yin and create a bare desert. The yin forces are fecund, but in excess become rank, and create dangerous swamps and jungles choked with creepers: the yin supports life, but in excess supports fevers and diseases, too. A yin force, beneficial and positive if before and

A fine village door, with hand-carved granite jambs and headstone, hand-painted frescoes and a well carved eavesboard. Both the fresco and the eavesboard are full of symbols of good fortune and happiness, bringing their benevolent influence to all who enter the door.

Most villages are built facing the best possible fung shui direction, with all the houses in a straight line. From the hills behind flows the yang force, on the flat land in front the yin force gathers. All the doors face the yin fields; the backs of the houses are protected from excessive flows of the yang forces by the fung shui wood.

MA MEI HA   RICHARD ABRAHALL

Some villages were founded on relatively poor fung shui sites. At Ma Mei Ha, the fung shui direction in front of the village was weak, and required protecting by a large pond and a thick fung shui grove. Often spirit trees associated with huge boulders protect vital fung shui directions.

SPIRIT TREE, LAM TSUEN   JANET STOTT

SPIRIT TREE AND BOULDERS, PAK MONG   RICHARD STOTT

The dead, once the bones have been cleaned and placed in an urn, are a beneficial fung shui force. The graves of the main clan ancestors are large and imposing. The urns of other villagers are housed less splendidly.

FUNG SHUI GRAVE, SHA LO TUNG, LEI UK   RICHARD ABRAHALL

FUNG SHUI GRAVE, SHA LO TUNG, LEI UK   KIM APLIN

BONE-URN STANDS, PAK MONG, TAI HO SAN TSUEN   KIM APLIN

below a site, would be harmful to humans if above and behind. A yang force, on the other hand, should approach a site from above and behind, vigorously but not violently.

The crucial fung shui task, therefore, is to identify the optimum fung shui site within an area. At this site the yin and the yang should be in the right relationship with the site and each other. Neither force should be in excess. At the same time, a stagnant site, where the powers are in absolute equilibrium, must be avoided; there must be a gentle flow of power through the site, and the settlement must face precisely along the line of flow. This produces the optimum situation for the fields, which would be below the point of equilibrium, in the yin area (all things with roots are by nature yin and require a yin area for optimum growth, but ideally one close to the point of inflow of the fertilising yang power), and also the optimum situation for the village, which would be above the point of equilibrium, in the yang area (all free moving things are by nature yang and require a yang area for optimum growth, but one also influenced by an adjacent life sustaining yin area).

The identification of an ideal site and the calculation of the flow of forces through it requires consideration of the relationship of the site to the surrounding hills, passes, ridges, streams and pools, which reflect the surrounding balance of yin and yang. The relationship to the stars and the earth's magnetic field are important, too, as the earth is only part of the greater cosmos, and the greater cosmos also influences individual locations.

At any site those flows of the forces which, in the context of that site, are beneficial, are called "hei" ("breath"), while those which are negative, are called "shat" ("death-bringing"). Negative flows can often be countered (for instance, a thick planting of trees can slow down an excessive yang flow; dams can slow down an excessive outflow of yin, or drainage works speed up an excessively slow yin outflow).

Eventually, the calculation of the fung shui of a site results in a determination of the most auspicious location and arrangement of a village, house or grave, and the best way of countering any negative forces influencing the site. It is believed that by placing oneself, or one's ancestors, in the optimum fung shui situation, good fortune, fertility, peace and a long life will come to both oneself and one's descendants. Peace of mind and contentment follow naturally from living where the forces of life are in a benign relationship. Fung shui is a practical philosophy if one accepts that humanity is part of a natural world order into which the fortunes of all men and women are interwoven, and where individuals are only able to overcome the life-forces surrounding them to a small degree.

The practicality of rural fung shui in terms of its impact on the cultural landscape of the New Territories may be understood when one realizes that the ideal village fung shui layout is similar to that needed for the growing of rice, which until about twenty years ago was the main occupation of the New Territories farming villages. In fact, the historical development of fung shui is thought to have gone hand in hand with the development of lowland rice farming. Both rice cultivation and fung shui ideally require small lowland valleys surrounded on three sides by hills which provide a controllable source of water from small hillside streams (vast rivers, too great to control, are undesirable). The many streams recommended by fung shui, and their meandering across the valley floor, would, if controlled, improve the potential for rice fields. The presence of many small streams also serves to control the flow of water during periods of intense summer rainfall. As in fung shui, water moving through the rice fields should not become stagnant, or move too quickly. A steady, gentle flow is needed. The constant flow of water helps to ensure a continuous supply of nutrients which, paralleling the life-giving hei of fung shui, should be allowed to penetrate the soil.

The weirs and channelled streams required for rice farming, and demanded for optimum fung shui effect, can still be seen in the fields of many villages, such as at Hok Tau Wai, near Fanling, which is now the only place in Hong Kong where rice is still grown, at the organic farm behind the village.

Classic statements of fung shui suggest that the ideal orientation is for the village to face south, in order to receive longer periods of sunlight and warmth resulting in increased rice yields. Southerly breezes would also provide some relief from the humidity of the summer months. The sun is regarded as the quintessence of the yang force. In the north, under the influence of the icy "black dragon" (hak lung), maximising the sun's influence is obviously desirable. In the south, however, the fiery "red bird" (chue tseuk) dominates, and increasing the sun's power would not be wise (who would wish to increase Hong Kong's summer heat?). In fung shui excess is always to be avoided. For this reason there is no preference for a south facing direction in this part of China. For instance, in Sha Tin, of more than 60 indigenous villages, only 2 or 3 face even approximately south, the great majority of villages facing south-east or north-west in accordance with the generally north-east to south-west aspect of the mountains.

A village should ideally be sited on raised ground at the back of the "armchair" valley. This site is called in fung shui "the dragon's lair". This is the most favourable point in the landscape, where the "white tiger" (pak fu) ridge joins the "green dragon" (tsing lung) ridge: the ridges running along either side of the village. At this point the houses are located above the valley floor and the risk of flooding is reduced. Valuable rice-land is not taken up with houses and outbuildings. Protection from cold winter winds is provided by the hills, which should be behind the village. The drier ridge slopes are generally unsuited to wet-rice growing and it is there that the village graves and friut trees are found.

Bad influences are thought to travel in straight lines. Protective ridges, groves of trees, clumps of bamboo and meandering lines in the landscape, such as local roads, all of which block or deflect these influences, are therefore desirable. Gaps between hills, especially where the opening directly faces the village, straight roads, or inlets of the sea pointing towards the village, and especially to its ancestral hall, channel evil forces (including cold, salt-laden winds or typhoons). Such situations are therefore to be avoided. Also to be avoided are views of earth graves (which being the first stage of burial are an ever present reminder of mortality), and also very steep slopes (where the yang force is likely to be excessively violent, and which might also be subject to landslips). It is for these reasons that some villages may have a fung shui wood to one side or in front of the village, or possibly may have several fung shui woods, to provide protection from dangerous forces deriving from the directions blocked by the woods.

In the mountainous landscape of the New Territories, with frequent views of the sea, the screening and deflection of undesirable sightlines from the ancestral hall, and the keeping open of favourable ones, provides the main reason why woods, groves, lines of trees

and even individual trees and clumps of bamboo are sited where they are, and why they are traditionally protected. The seemingly random scatter of woods and trees in the landscape falls into a logical pattern once one understands the basics of fung shui. They help to form an almost "sacred landscape" unique to south China.

Within the New Territories, the best village sites were already occupied by the Punti (Cantonese speaking clans) by the time that the Hakka people came into the region at the end of the seventeenth and the beginning of the eighteenth century and these latecomers had to make do with village sites that may not have been optimum from the fung shui point of view. It is at these less than ideal late settled sites that the influence of fung shui can most easily be seen through the efforts made by the villagers to screen and deflect the undesirable forces of the area.

Thus, where a path leaves such a village, especially where it crosses a stream or the end of a fung shui wood, the site is often associated with a clump of bamboo, a large rock or a large camphor or banyan tree, or sometimes all three. Such a site is "the mouth of water", (the flow of the path symbolizing water), and the bamboo, rock, or tree is the fung shui "guardian star" which defends the village against excessive outflow of hei.

In a typical fusion of fung shui with animist beliefs, an earth god is sometimes thought to dwell in this guardian star tree or rock, at the foot of which is often found a shrine where the earth god can be worshipped. Where such a site adjoins a fung shui wood, the earth god is believed to roam about in the sanctuary of the wood, but its home is in the guardian tree, which in fung shui terms is even more important than the woodland itself. In most villages the siting of the earth god shrines, even

if not associated with a guardian star fung shui site, is closely connected with the village's fung shui, with the earth-god shrines protecting and reinforcing the most important fung shui points within the immediate village area.

The banyan tree is the most frequently encountered fung shui tree, as its profuse production of berries and the tenacity of its roots symbolises fertility and perseverance in the face of adversity. The camphor tree is also a favoured fung shui species as its camphor impregnated wood is almost immune to decay and has come to symbolise incorruptability and immortality.

The planting of a grove of trees and bamboo behind the village with a ming tong pond in front, is the typical form of village fung shui. The grove supports the mountain star at the rear of the village, bringing good health and many sons. The pond supports the water star bringing wealth to the village and also serving many practical functions, including irrigation, washing, fire-fighting and raising fish. The construction of such a pond would have been expensive for a small village and they are not very common in the New Territories. Few Hakka villages have a pond, making do with the flooded rice fields in front of the village instead. Most Ming-Tong ponds are now either dry or have been filled in but fine examples may still be found at Fanling Wai, Ma Tseuk Leng, Lin Ma Hang, and at Ha Wo Hang in front of the newly restored ancestral hall.

The small fung shui woods behind the villages also have practical functions. Partly linked to fung shui, the practice of cleaning hillside graves twice a year during the Ching Ming and Chung Yeung festivals in April and October respectively, results in much burning of hillsides which causes ash and soil enriched with worm casts to be washed down to the fields below, possibly providing a source of fertilizer for the rice. By recommending a stand of trees and vegetation behind and upslope of the village, fung shui protects the village from landslips and prevents the soil and ash from being washed into the village after the rains. As the fung shui woods are usually resistant to burning, they also act as an effective firebreak.

Fung shui woods also protect the village from cold or salt-laden winds, and also from the worst effects of summer typhoons. At the same time, by cooling the breezes that blow through them, fung shui woods also provide a form of natural air conditioning to the village during the humid summer months. On flat land the fung shui wood takes the place of the protecting hill to the rear of the village, in which case it is often a narrow symbolic belt of banyans and bamboo as all the available land was formerly needed for farming.

The trees in fung shui woods are normally allowed to grow naturally without any cutting or pruning. Where a tree is needed for the carving of a new image for the village temple, then a camphor tree from the fung shui wood is, with appropriate ceremonial, cut. Travelling carvers select a suitable tree, and, after felling, it is seasoned for a few years before the carver returns to complete his work. The gathering of wood from the trees for other purposes is, however, prohibited by the village elders, although in some villages dead wood may be collected from the ground. Firewood, gathered from outside the fung shui wood, is still used in many villages by the older people as it is cheaper than buying bottled gas. Fung shui woods are also a rich source of medicinal plants and herbs which are still sometimes gathered by the old ladies of the village as home remedies for common ailments.

The fung shui woods themselves are of native broadleaved evergreen trees, although fruit trees, such as Lychee, or Longan, are occasionally planted on the edge of the wood near the village. Such fruit trees are almost always owned by individual families, although im some villages, such as those in Pat Heung, anyone from the village may gather fruit from trees within the fung shui wood for their own use. Some fruit tree species, such as the longan, have traditional culinary, medicinal or timber uses. A common tree in fung shui woods is the incense tree, or heung, from which incense sticks were made. The wood of this tree gave its name to Hong Kong ("Heung Kong": "Incense Harbour") since Hong Kong was, many centuries ago, a port from which the scented wood was exported. Heung trees were formerly grown in plantations and it is unlikely that trees from within a fung shui wood would ever have been cut for their timber. Although stands of bamboo within a fung shui wood would not normally be cut, this plant, of course, lends itself to a myriad of village uses. Bamboo was often planted at the ends of a fung shui wood to provide better fung shui protection yet not obstruct too much light. There was often a narrow cleared space kept between the fung shui wood and the rear of the village to keep snakes and vermin away from the village and to ensure that tall trees would not be a threat to the houses themselves in a typhoon.

Floristically, most fung shui groves contain a diversity of tree species characteristic of local natural woodland. In fact, it is often unclear which came first, the wood or the village. Certainly, most fung shui woods on flat land, such as those around the Yuen Long villages, were planted and are mostly longan orchards, as there was little dry ground otherwise available for fruit trees. Other seemingly natural fung shui woods were also planted by the ancestors when the village was founded three or four hundred years ago, such as those at Lin Au and Hang Ha Po near Tai Po and at Pat Heung where the wood was specifically planted for shelter from the winds. However, tradition maintains that some of the woods behind villages at the foot of a hillslope may be derived from the earlier forest, for instance at Sheung Ling Pei on north Lantau, and at Sheung Wo Hang and Ma Tseuk Leng near Sha Tau Kok, and at Hok Tau Wai, where the village tradition is that space for the village was carved out of the forest when the village was founded over two hundred years ago, with the remaining forest left as fung shui woodland. These woods, and a handful of other fung shui woods, such as that belonging to the abandoned village at Shing Mun, and the wood opposite South Island school on Nam Fung road, (which is the oldest remaining wood on Hong Kong Island and may have been the fung shui wood for the former Little Hong Kong village), contain a great diversity of tree species. These include the rare Chinese Endospermum, which is only found in woods older than 150 years. These woods give some indication of the nature of woodlands in Hong Kong in former times. Although it is unlikely that they are remnants of the original tropical monsoon forest which was probably cleared centuries ago, they are at least well-established and fully regenerated woods, and may have a core of natural forest features.

Over 300 major fung shui woods have been recorded in Hong Kong as a whole, and with total area over 700 hectares they are our largest resource of native trees and are characteristic features of the landscape of the New Territories. They are also important for sheltering some of our larger mammals, such as civet, porcupine and wild boar.

Until recent decades, fung shui woods were almost the only native woods to be found, since other trees, not protected by fung shui demands, had long since been cut for fuel. Since the electrification of the villages grass and fuel-wood are no longer regularly cut from the hillsides. This has allowed the fung shui woods to spread out across the previously grass-covered hills, so that now there is probably more natural woodland in Hong Kong than there has been for centuries.

As we have seen, fung shui has a sound practical basis and formed a system of beliefs which guided the development of a land use system which was based on the most appropriate pattern of land use for rice farming. Fung shui represents an environmentally sound system of site planning which organizes the various elements of the rural Chinese landscape in a way that maintains the traditional agricultural economy and the environment.

By providing a guide to the optimum farming system for rice production, fung shui contributes to the fertility and wealth of the land and its people. There is of course, a great deal more to fung shui than this, but the practical analogy does provide a suitable frame of reference for the secular mind to grasp. It is possible to think of the fung shui belief system as a strategy for settlement, subsistence and landscape interpretation and modification for the purposes of rice farming. In other words, local rural fung shui may be thought of as a "pattern language" in which proper management of the environment, and proper settlement behaviour, could be understood, remembered and passed on in a traditional rural society.

However, looking at the New Territories today, with its abandoned rice fields and spreading rash of container storage depots, one may ask, "If fung shui enabled the evolution of a productive and harmonious landscape, why is that landscape being ruined so thoroughly today?" The quick answer is that money means more to many present day New

Territories villagers than does fung shui. However, the truth lies partly within fung shui itself.

With the growth of the new towns in the New Territories in the 1970's, many villagers either gave up farming for an easier life in the towns or emigrated overseas. The final blow was in the late 1970's when rice began to be imported more cheaply from mainland China than it could be grown at home. Rather than turning to market gardening themselves, the villagers either leased their land to immigrant farmers or abandoned it completely. In traditional Chinese rural society the rice growing land is owned by the clan and the activities associated with the growing of rice are full of social and community reinforcing values. However, the growing of vegetables by individual farmers has no social prestige, so if rice could not be grown, the land was abandoned.

If the farmland becomes abandoned, much of the detail of the fung shui rules required to be observed goes with it. There is nothing in the traditional rules to state what the fung shui implications of container depots or car-dumps are. Within the traditional, rice-growing society of the past, observance of fung shui rules led to a noticeably well-planned landscape of great natural beauty, with villages, woods, hills and fields forming a balanced and coherent whole; one in which it was indeed possible to live with peace of mind and tranquility. Unfortunately, the rules of fung shui seem to be ineffective in fending off the worst effects of our modern age.

Richard Webb is a former Landscape Architect at the Architectural Services Department.

GATEHOUSE WITH EARTHGOD SHRINE, SAN UK TSAI   JANET STOTT

EARTHGOD SHRINE, MA MEI HA   RICHARD ABRAHALL

SPIRIT TREE AND SHRINE, PAK MONG   RICHARD STOTT

SPIRIT TREE AND SHRINE, PAK MONG   RICHARD STOTT

Where paths enter villages, an earth god shrine is usually found. These are sometimes just a stone or a trough of earth at the foot of a tree, but are often more elaborate structures of brick and stone, although still often built near the tree which is the real home of the deity.

EARTHGOD SHRINE AND SPIRIT TREE IN A *FUNG SHUI* GROVE, SHEUNG WO HANG   RICHARD ABRAHALL

"Virtuous like the male ancestors, loving like the female ancestors" - ancestors, deities and the fung shui forces of nature, this is the villagers' world.

CHAPTER THREE

VILLAGE FESTIVALS

SHA LO TUNG, CHEUNG UK   KIM APLIN

VILLAGE FESTIVALS

P. H. HASE

The villagers of the New Territories led a generally hard-working and frugal existence dominated by the demands of their rice-crops. However, traditional life was not one of un-relieved labour. The New Territories village life was punctuated by seasonal and occasional festivals, which brought colour and excitement into villagers' lives, and the occasional holiday from field work. Many of these traditional festivals are still observed by village communities today.

The villagers traditionally lived in a society of which the spirits of the dead, and the spirits of the water and the earth, were as much a part as the villagers living in the village houses. A successful and peaceful life demanded that the villagers remained on amicable and polite terms with all their neighbours, both their fellow villagers, and the spirits of the village. Basic good manners required a villager to pay his respects to his neighbours at their weddings, first moon festivals, and funerals: equally, basic good manners required a villager to pay his respects at appropriate seasons to the village dead, and the local earth and water gods.

On the last day of the year, every family would paste up at their doors lucky papers, including couplets provided by village scholars. The village elders would similarly paste up lucky couplets, on behalf of the villagers at large, at the doors of the ancestral hall, on the pillars of the earth-god shrines, and, where there was a temple near the village, on the door-posts of the temple as well. Where the earth-god had no shrine, but was worshipped at the foot of a great tree or rock, then the elders would decorate the tree or rock with strips of red paper. These traditions are still observed in most villages.

On the first day of the New Year, the village unicorn or lion dance will, in many villages,

visit every household. The team is welcomed with fire-crackers at the door before passing on to the next household.

While traditions differed from village to village, sometimes markedly, it was normal that, on the second day of the New Year, a villager would first of all pay respects to the immediate family members, and would light incense and bow to pay respects to the family's immediate ancestors at the family ancestral altar. It was and is the practice in many villages for all the heads of families to follow this by going early in the morning to pay their respects to the ancestors in the ancestral hall. After paying respects to the ancestors, the heads of families will also go to pay respects to the village earthgods. Later, the villagers go to pay their respects to more distant relatives. In the bigger Punti villages this New Year ceremonial at the ancestral hall is often conducted with considerable ceremonial and solemnity.

At an agreed date during the first few days of the New Year the villagers would also, in many villages, pay further, communal, respects to the earth and water spirits. Many villages still have an elder who knows how to chant the long invitations to the spirits to attend the forthcoming ceremonies. The elder will chant these invitations to the spirits during the morning. In Hakka villages a pig, or, in larger villages, two pigs, would have been reared at the expense of the villagers at large - in some villages, the rearing of the pig was rotated round the village families, in others, small pieces of land had been set aside, the income from which provided for the pig. This pig was sacrificed to the earth-gods later in the morning, a ritual still conducted in a few places, although today the pig is more likely to be bought following a collection of cash from villages families.

In those Hakka villages which follow this tradition, this New Year pig is washed down on the chosen day and tied alive to a bamboo pole, and then carried in procession with the village elders and the village unicorn team to the earth-god and water-spirit shrines, in front of each of which the pig is offered while the elders pay their respects to the spirit by bowing and offering incense. Finally the procession reaches the senior earth-god shrine. There the village elders cut off the pig's ear, or slit it, catching the blood in a bowl. While the elders pay their respects as solemnly as they can, the blood is sprinkled over the shrine, while the elders beseech the earth-god to continue to protect and preserve the village. The pig is then taken back to the village in procession, slaughtered, and chopped up. The meat is then parboiled under the supervision of the elders, and distributed to each village family, for whom it constitutes the main meal of the day. Villagers living away from the village will, if at all possible, return for this meal. By eating this meat, the villagers link themselves to the ceremony at the earth-god shrine, and bring the preserving power of the earth-god into their home.

In the Punti villages, the New Year pig is more often associated with the ceremonial at the Ancestral Hall, and the meat is often distributed to the villagers in an uncooked state after the carcase of the animal has been offered to the ancestors. In these villages, the worship at the earth-god shrines is often conducted less formally than in the Hakka villages. In both, however, the New Year sees the villagers paying respects, not just to living relatives, but also to the dead and the village spirits.

Where a village family has had a son born to it during the previous year, the head of the family makes a special offering to the ancestors

Fierce door gods turn away ill fortune, and couplets wish the true happiness of peace, and such wealth as heaven permits, to those who enter, and, above all, vast happiness.

HUNG LENG TEMPLE   RICHARD ABRAHALL

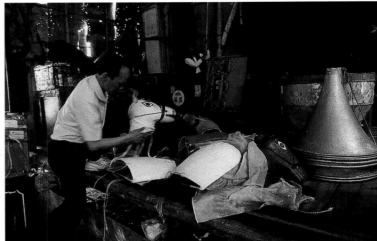

AT THE LUNG YEUK TAU TA TSIU   RICHARD ABRAHALL

All village communities have their own temple. The Hung Leng Temple serves the villages in the Lau Shui Heung area. Every year villagers will come to worship on the god's birthday. At Lung Yeuk Tau, as in many village areas, the special ritual of the Ta Tsiu is held to worship all the gods once every ten years.

Earth gods, well gods, the major and minor deities from the local temples, and any other deities worshipped by villagers are invited to a temporary temple where they are worshipped by all the people. For the amusement of both gods and men, operas are put on in a temporary matshed hall.

AT THE LUNG YEUK TAU TA TSIU   RICHARD ABRAHALL

AT THE LUNG YEUK TAU TA TSIU   RICHARD ABRAHALL

of a lantern hung in the Ancestral Hall. The head of the family will often also attend with the elders at the procession to the earth-god shrines. This brings the new child formally to the attention of the ancestors and earth spirits, and is parallel to the formal notice of the child's birth sent to other village families at the time of the child's First Moon feast.

These New Year customs and rituals make the point very powerfully that the dead and the living, humans and spirits, all form a single coherent whole, with all equally involved in the New Year festivities.

The ancestors are not worshipped only at the New Year. The elders, especially in Punti villages, also often hold formal ceremonies in the ancestral hall in the Autumn, similar to those at the New Year. Respects are also paid to the dead at the Ching Ming and Chung Yeung Tomb Festivals, in the Spring and Autumn respectively.

At Ching Ming and Chung Yeung the dead are worshipped at their tombs, rather than at the Ancestral Hall or the family ancestral altar. At these festivals, the clan as a whole first worships at the tombs of the high clan ancestors, and then the individual families worship at the tombs of the ancestors of their own descent line. Many villagers have a dozen or more tombs which they are required to visit, and up to four or five days is required to complete the round, given that villager graves are often scattered over the mountains in sites difficult of access. Practicalities are used to reduce the burden - brothers and cousins will, for instance, often agree among themselves a distribution, with each ancestor being wor-shipped by one on behalf of the whole group. For the high clan ancestors, where basic good manners demand that a reasonably large group attend, many villages have a rota system whereby each year a separate group of families is required to attend. Pork is distributed to those who turn up, an inducement which was very

real in the past, when a family feast of meat was a rare treat. For some villages, where high clan ancestors are buried in very remote and difficult sites, just one or two villagers chosen by lot make the journey to the tomb on behalf of all the rest. But if a tomb is neglected entirely, this would be the worst of bad manners, and would lead to the ancestor in question becoming justly angered with his descendants, with incalculable consequences.

Paying respects at the tomb consists of tidying up the grave, cutting back wild grasses, and repainting inscriptions as needed. The villagers bow before the tomb, and then eat a meal at the graveside. The villagers say that what they do at the tomb is the same that they would do to an elderly living relative - if they visited such a relative, they would help tidy the house, or do any necessary work in the house beyond the relative's strength, and would show that they still held the relative in respect, before eating a meal with them.

In some New Territories villages there are Hero Shrines, dedicated to those young men of the village or district who died in some inter-village war in the past. Normally, these young heroes died before they married, since the burden of village defence always fell on the younger men. As such, they have no descendants to pay them respects. Normally, dying without descendants is considered the worst of unfilial acts, but the villagers traditionally viewed these heroes as having shown "real filial piety" by dying to preserve their village. The village or district elders, therefore, usually worship these heroes twice a year on behalf of the villagers as a whole, in the Spring and Autumn.

At a few places "uncared-for bones" - the bodies of people dying without relatives in a village area - were buried by the elders, and are also worshipped annually, to avoid the spirits of the dead causing trouble by being ignored.

Apart from the ancestors, and the purely local earth and water spirits, the villagers also recognise that the gods should be worshipped appropriately, since the gods, too, are part of the village society. Erection and maintenance of a temple was an expensive undertaking, and only the wealthiest villages could afford one - normally, a temple was the joint responsibility of all the villages of a district. The deity in the temple was perceived by the villagers as their representative before the whole community of the deities, a point made explicit in some temples, where boards with the name and titles of all the major gods are to be found as well as the statue of the deity to whom the temple is dedicated, so that any worship, while specifically to the major deity, is at the same time to all the other gods.

The gods are worshipped whenever a family feels that problems have arisen beyond the capacity of the village and its spirits to cope with, or where a villager feels he needs the advice and assistance of the deity in making some major decision. In the past, serious illness, childlessness, and help in making decisions on matters such as a building a new house, going into business, marriage, or such like, were the most likely reasons why a villager would seek the assistance of the deity: today, business problems are more frequent. The deity normally offers advice, as generally in the South China region, through the casting of "tsim", the fortune sticks kept in bamboo containers on the altar.

No villager, however, feels that the deities are likely to be forthcoming if approached only in need. If the villager does not pay respects to the deity when times are good, his bad manners can only lead to difficulties if he is forced to go to the temple in bad times. Heads of families, and village elders especially, will go, therefore, to pay their respects at the god's birthday, and the whole community will mount birthday celebrations for the deity, at the least with decorations at the temple, but with opera performances where there is enough money for this. In the past, a feast was often held by the elders in front of the temple at the god's birthday: the deity was always considered to be the unseen guest at such feasts. Such feasts are nowadays less frequent, because of the absence of so many of the elders from the area on business, but several are still held, although possibly in a nearby restaurant rather than in front of the temple. Once again, the villagers view their relationship with the deities as being based on good manners - it is only good manners to be respectful and polite to those who you feel you may one day want to act on your behalf.

During the agricultural year there are a number of obvious nodal points, at the harvests, and following the transplanting of the rice crops. Seasonal feasts marked these points in the year. The fields were cleared of all crops and left empty for the 15 days of the New Year: transplanting of the rice seedlings started as soon as the New Year was over. Completion of this task was marked by Ching Ming, about six weeks later. Tuen Ng (the Dragon-boat Festival) marked the start of the harvest period for the first rice crop, and the beginning of the heaviest work in the fields, which was ended by the Mid-Autumn Festival, by when the second rice crop should have been successfully trans-planted. Chung Yeung marked the beginning of the second rice harvest: the fields should have been cleared of rice and re-planted with the winter crops before the Winter Solstice Festival.

Every family celebrated these turning points of the year with a family feast. Even the poorest of families would have bought meat for these festival dinners. For some families in the past, these festival meals, and the meals they were invited to when neighbours married or were buried, were the only times they ate meat: for wealthier families, these festival meals were

when the family would make an effort to have better than normal food - a chicken for instance, or some spirits from the market-town distillery. Special festival food, such as New Year turnip pudding, steamed sweet buns, or rice dumplings, were prepared for these festivals, and were often given by richer families to their poorer neighbours as a gesture of neighbour-liness. While these feasts were usually a matter for individual families, it was common for cousins to join together to allow for a more jovial affair. Today, most village families still hold these seasonal feasts.

Sometimes these festival meals were celebrated with traditional entertainments, such as the ritual theft of vegetables by unmarried youths for the evening meal of the 15th day of the New Year, story-telling and the singing of Mountain Songs (especially at the Mid-Autumn Festival), or, for some villages near the sea, the boat-races of the Dragon-boat Festival. Youngsters would sometimes hold seances to contact the dead (a feature of the Mid-Autumn Festival). Many villages, especially the Hakka ones, prepared free-flying hot-air balloons for the fun of it, also at the Mid-Autumn Festival. Often the festival meals would take place late in the evening, by torch-light, and were followed the next day by the luxury of a later than normal start to the day.

Weddings were usually held in the slack periods of the agricultural year, because they too were a whole-village celebration. By tradition, the family of any bridegroom was obliged to invite the whole village to the wedding feast. Normally, this same tradition of inviting the whole village was also followed for funeral feasts, first moon feasts (at least for sons), and the feasts held to celebrate the completion of a new house. In fact, it was, in the past, and even to some degree now, difficult to hold a village feast unless the whole village was invited, since the mounting of a feast required the assistance of most of the young

men of the village, and they would not co-operate unless their families were invited.

Village feasts required pigs to be slaughtered and prepared, large quantities of foodstuffs to be carried on shoulder-poles back to the village from the market town perhaps six or seven miles away across the hills, and special temporary stoves to be built on a suitable site, and protected from rain by a canopy of mats. Vast quantities of vegetables and other foodstuffs had to be cut up and prepared while still fresh. Many buckets of water had to be drawn from the village well, and carried to the cooking site until several of the village threshing vats were full. Tables and stools (most villages owned a set of these communally for use in feasts) had to be carried from the village store and set up. The village's communally owned bowls had to be washed, and set out. Those villagers who knew how to cook festival food in large quantity had to be ready to cook for several hours. All families to be invited had to be personally informed, for reasons of good manners. All in all, a village feast required several dozen helpers. These feasts, which are still today held here and there, were, in the past, one of the most potent forces building up the strong feeling of social coherence which has always so marked the New Territories villages.

Traditional weddings and funerals could also only be carried out with the support of the village as a whole. Carrying the wedding sedan-chair, and providing a suitably impressive escort of flag-carriers and pole-bearers on the one hand, and carrying the coffin and digging the grave on the other, required the services of all the young men of even a moderately large village, to say nothing of the feast that accompanied every wedding and funeral. While traditional weddings are a thing of the past, traditional funerals can still occasionally be seen in the New Territories villages.

By far the most important village festival,

LUNG YEUK TAU TA TSIU, THE KING OF HELL   RICHARD ABRAHALL

LENG PEI TSUEN   KIM APLIN

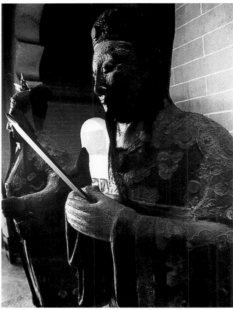

HUNG LENG TEMPLE   RICHARD ABRAHALL

NEAR SHA LO TUNG, LEI UK   ANDY DOMERACKI

A feature of the Ta Tsiu is the huge paper and rattan statue of the King of Hell, the controller of ghosts. The climax of the ritual is the burning of the statue late at night on the last night of the festival. Within the community temple the deity is placed in a richly decorated niche, with attendant deities on either side in front. On the altar and offering table are offerings of tea and fruit, paper flowers, incense and candles.

HUNG LENG TEMPLE   RICHARD ABRAHALL

however, was and is the Ta Tsiu. The Ta Tsiu is one of the two routine occasions when the villagers use teams of Taoist priests (called by the villagers Nam Mo Lo) - the other occasion being the traditional funeral. The various participants in the Ta Tsiu have different views as to what the purpose of the rituals is. For the Taoist priests the Ta Tsiu is the most sacred of all rituals, and aims to restore the proper balance of the cosmos: the central rite is calling down the power of the three high gods of Taoism, using written texts handed down through generations of Taoist priests, to a cleansed and purified site, to bring the great structure of the universe into the perfect balance typified by the Yin-Yang symbol.

For village scholars, and to those village elders who have studied the gods, the ritual aims at bringing the villagers back into a proper relationship with the deities: the central rite is the gathering into one place of objects representing all the gods, and their worship by all the villagers, thus renewing the villagers' relationship with them. To these village scholars the rituals of the Taoist priests are designed to cleanse and purify an area in which all the gods can be worshipped safely, and to drive out and keep under control any evil spirits which might otherwise interfere with the worship of the deities.

For the ordinary villagers, the rituals are designed to placate, control, and remove from the village area evil spirits and the ghosts of those dead not cared for by their descendants: for these villagers the central rite is the erection of a gigantic statue of the King of Hell, and the burning of the statue on the last night of the rites, whereby the King of Hell returns to his own place, carrying with him the ill-disposed and troublesome spirits. To these villagers the Taoist priests are magicians, whose duty it is to control the spirits, by inducing them all to gather at the same place, and then forcing them to accept the bonds

placed on them by the King of Hell.

These varying views of the Ta Tsiu ritual in the New Territories make the ritual particularly complex. In some parts of the ritual, the Taoist priests act on their own, in others with a group of villagers representing the whole community, and in yet others with the whole village community in close attendance. In other parts of the ritual, the villagers act on their own, without the attendance of the Taoists, sometimes in accordance with instructions issued by the villagers' own ritual experts.

In the New Territories, the holding of a Ta Tsiu usually requires five days and nights of more or less continuous ritual activity, not counting several shorter periods several months earlier when certain preliminary rituals are required to be carried out. The Ta Tsiu is always held in the winter, when the weather is cooler, but the actual date is chosen by the deities through the casting of tsim. The conduct of the ritual requires a ritual area to be marked out and several temporary buildings to be built on it. A temporary temple to the three high gods of Taoism, with quarters for the Taoist priests and their attendant musicians, forms one of these temporary bamboo structures. A further temporary temple, in which objects representing all the deities are placed, is another: usually this is built next to a temporary office for the organisers, and an open-fronted room for greeting guests. A kitchen for cooking vegetarian food is off to one side, since only vegetarian food is allowed during the period of the rituals. Along one side of the site a bamboo wall is erected, on which the name-list of all the involved villagers is pasted for the deities and spirits to take note of. A tall structure houses the statue of the King of Hell: often the statue is over 20 feet high. Finally, in the centre of the site is an opera matshed. Opera is put on to keep the spirits happen until their removal by the King of Hell, but the villagers greatly love the opera, and the matshed is

always full. Since nothing must be done to interfere with the spirits' free passage into the opera matshed, the matshed has to be open-sided. Listening to the opera, therefore, is free to villagers, at least if the villager is prepared to stand.

The Ta Tsiu is so complex that a full description of the rituals would take a whole book. However, a few of the more important rituals should be noted. At the beginning of the main period of ritual, the Taoist priests purify and sanctify the ritual area, and announce themselves to the three high gods of Taoism and to the Jade Emperor, seeking approval for the holding of the rites. This ritual is considered important by both the Taoists and the villagers. The villagers have a purification ritual of their own which is carried out during the ritual period: a few seeds, representing the impurities of the house, are taken out of each house and carried away to be burnt by a villager deputed to do this. Another vital rite carried out during the ritual period is the Hang Heung, or procession of the Taoist priests around the district, to bring the purity and power of the Ta Tsiu to every corner of the district. The villagers view this rite very seriously: in the late nineteenth century the villagers of Tai Po Mei left the Sha Tin Kau Yeuk alliance of villages because Tai Po Mei was omitted from the Hang Heung since it was so far from the Ta Tsiu ground.

The villagers seek out every god or spirit worshipped within the area holding the Ta Tsiu. Normally the area supporting a Ta Tsiu will also support a temple. The carrying-statue of the temple god will be brought solemnly to the site in a sedan chair carried by the elders, and placed in the centre of the temporary altar. The other important gods are often represented by one or two boards with their names and titles: these boards are placed next to the carrying-statue of the local god. Occasionally other deities are represented by small statues. All the earth and water spirits of the area, and the spirits of numinous trees, rocks and springs, are invited: these spirits are often invited to take as a temporary habitation small red flags stuck into suitable stands (often half potatoes are used). Specialist gods worshipped by local martial arts instructors, doctors, or shopkeepers are sought out and invited in. Normally a villager will worship only a few gods and spirits: the bringing of all these gods and spirits to one place allows the villagers to pay his respects to those he would normally neglect. The invitation to these gods and spirits, and the setting up of the temporary altar with them all on it, is conducted by the villagers on their own, and the attendant rituals are not usually assisted by the Taoist priests.

Once the temporary temple of all the gods is set up, then every family worships there. Usually, each family head, or his wife, will worship there once each day of the festival. The elders of each village in the area worship each day, accompanied by their village lion or unicorn team.

Another ritual, of the greatest significance to the villagers, but conducted for them by the Taoist priests is the reading out of the name list. This is read several times, on different dates, and the list is eventually burnt. All this has two purposes for the villagers. Firstly, the list, which includes the names of all the villagers, is a ritual proof of the all-inclusive nature of the rituals. If any villagers' names are omitted, this would leave a hole in the area purified through which some of the evil spirits could evade the King of Hell. The village elders are, therefore, very careful to check that all their villagers are included, and that the writing of their names is correct. Secondly, the appearance of a name on the list is proof that a villager is accepted as a villager. Outsiders resident in the area must also appear on the name-list, since they, too, must be covered by the rituals if the whole area is to be cleansed and protected, without any

dangerous gaps, but the names of outsiders are added in a separate section of the name-list, under a separate heading. The preparation of the name-list, therefore, takes several months, and sometimes involves the settling of disputes as to the legitimacy of doubtful births, or adoptions.

Another ritual conducted by the Taoists is the release of caged song-birds, to gain merit with the heavenly powers. The villagers consider that one of the ritual aims of the Ta Tsiu is to express the villagers' sorrow for their need to kill animals or fish to eat. This is the reason given by the villagers for the vegetarian food, and the release of the birds.

The final great ritual, at midnight on the last night of the rites, is the carrying of the statue of the King of Hell, and the troublesome spirits held captive in his stomach (which is appropriately huge) to a burning site outside the village. The villagers consider this a very anxious time. If the statue stops moving while being carried, some of the spirits might escape. At the burning site, any house towards which the statue faces while being burnt may be affected by the evil spirits "catching hold" of the building as they are driven off to Hell. Anyone present whose name is spoken aloud may find that the spirits similarly "catch hold" of the name to disastrous effect. Should the statue fall over, or collapse during the burning, this again might allow the spirits to escape. Outsiders are always warned to obey the rules, especially as to names, and the statue is always surrounded by the young men of the villages with long poles, which they use to push aside anything that might threaten to stop the statue's passage, and which they will later use to prop the statue up during the burning to ensure that it does not collapse or fall down.

The Ta Tsiu rituals were, and are, immensely expensive, and few areas can afford to hold them more than once every decade, although Cheung Chau manages to do so every year (the

Bun Festival is in fact a Ta Tsiu, with a few special features). Even today the Ta Tsiu functions without the slightest signs of declining significance for the village communities. Villagers living abroad all make great efforts to return for it, often in their hundreds.

The Ta Tsiu has always caused problems for Christian villagers. The other villagers find it essential to have the names of their Christian village brethren on the village name-list, but this is often objected to, particularly by certain fundamentalist groups. Villagers also sometimes feel that the Christian god should be placed on the altar to all the gods if any villagers are christian, for fear that the Christian god would be offended if the other villagers ignored him. This has never proved acceptable to any Christian groups. In the nineteenth century, these problems caused real difficulties in many areas of the region, although, in today's New Territories, compromises allow Christian and non-Christian villagers to co-exist within the Ta Tsiu community.

It will be obvious that Ta Tsiu is an immensely colourful event. In the past the Ta Tsiu, and the other village festivals and feasts, brought fantasy and colour in rich abundance to lives otherwise noticeably short of both. The village festivals, and especially the Ta Tsiu, remain the most colourful and vivid of spectacles, and give a contemporary glimpse of what a traditional festival meant to the villagers in the past, and to some degree, still means to the villagers of today.

Dr. P.H. Hase, is a Council member of the RAS. He came to Hong Kong in 1972 and has been researching into village life and history in the area for over twenty years. He has published extensively, especially in the Journal of the Society.

LUNG YEUK TAU, ANCESTRAL HALL   RICHARD ABRAHALL

For the period of the Ta Tsiu, ritual leaders are chosen from among the village men to
represent the village at all the religious rituals. During the period of the rituals they hold a
special place within the local society, and this is marked by the wearing of cheung sam.
These ritual leaders are preparing for a ritual to be held in the Ancestral Hall

LIN AU RICHARD ABRAHALL

THE NEW YEAR UNICORN,SHEUNG WO HANG
RICHARD ABRAHALL

THE NEW YEAR UNICORN VISITS
THE VILLAGE HOUSES, SHEUNG WO HANG
RICHARD ABRAHALL

WAITING FOR THE NEW YEAR UNICORN,
SHEUNG WO HANG RICHARD ABRAHALL

All rituals require lion or unicorn dances. Most villagers buy their lions or unicorns, not from shops in the city, but from villagers who have learnt the art of making them from their fathers and grandfathers. The Headman of Lin Au makes unicorns for most of the Hakka villages of the Tai Po area. He hopes his son and grandson, who are holding the completed unicorn, will learn the art from him. At the New Year the village unicorn dance team visits all the houses, and is greeted with firecrackers and lucky money.

TAOIST PRIEST, LUNG YEUK TAU TA TSIU
RICHARD ABRAHALL

RITUAL LEADERS, LUNG YEUK TAU TA TSIU
RICHARD ABRAHALL

OPERA SINGER, LUNG YEUK TAU TA TSIU
RICHARD ABRAHALL

CHIEF RITUAL LEADER, LUNG YEUK TAU TA TSIU
RICHARD ABRAHALL

AT THE TA TSIU, LUNG YEUK TAU
RICHARD ABRAHALL

The rituals of the Ta Tsiu are conducted by groups of taoist priests, or Nam Mo Lo. The leader of the priests who conduct most of the Ta Tsiu in the eastern New Territories has been following this profession for more than sixty years, following his father and grandfather. Whenever he is present before the altar of the deities he is accompanied by the chief ritual leader carrying a small shrine with a roll written with all the names of the participating villagers.

THE TAOIST ALTAR, LUNG YEUK TAU TA TSIU RICHARD ABRAHALL

TAOIST PRIESTS AND RITUAL LEADERS,
LUNG YEUK TAU TA TSIU RICHARD ABRAHALL

READING THE NAME-LIST, LUNG YEUK TAU TA TSIU RICHARD ABRAHALL

BLESSING THE NAME-LIST, LUNG YEUK TAU TA TSIU RICHARD ABRAHALL

BURNING THE NAME-LIST, LUNG YEUK TAU TA TSIU RICHARD ABRAHALL

At the Ta Tsiu one of the most important rituals is the reading out of the names of the participating villagers. This is done by the taoist priests but village representatives stand close by to ensure that no name is left out. After the name list is blessed and purified it is tied to the back of a paper horse and sent to the supreme deity in fire. At Lung Yeuk Tau this ritual takes place in front of the Ancestral Hall.

KAT HING WAI, KAM TIN
[ORIGINAL PLAN, OMITTING REDEVELOPMENT]

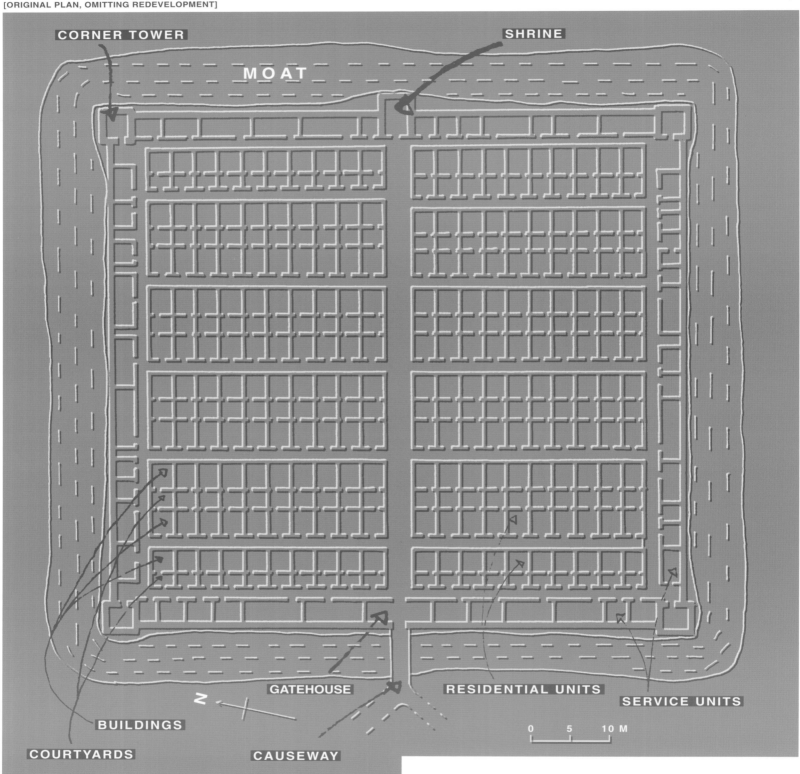

CORNER TOWER

SHRINE

MOAT

BUILDINGS

COURTYARDS

GATEHOUSE

RESIDENTIAL UNITS

SERVICE UNITS

CAUSEWAY

N

0 5 10 M

HONG KONG'S WAI:
DEFENSIVE ARCHITECTURE OF THE NEW TERRITORIES

LUNG YEUK TAU, MA WAT WAI   RICHARD ABRAHALL

HONG KONG'S WAI:

DEFENSIVE ARCHITECTURE OF THE NEW TERRITORIES

DAVID LUNG WITH ANN FRIEDMAN

Wai, means both "defense" and "surround." In the New Territories, "wai" has come to mean defended or fortified village. Such fortified villages take two main forms: villages composed of row houses occupied by family groups, often belonging to a single clan, and surrounded by a defensive wall, such as the three Kam Tin villages of Kat Hing Wai, Tai Hong Wai and Wing Lung Wai; and family compounds, owned by a single wealthy landowner, or by a few closely related men, where the residential units face into a central courtyard or courtyards, in such a way that the back walls of the residential units form a defensible wall, such as Shan Ha Wai (Tsang Tai Uk) in the Sha Tin Valley. In the New Territories today, not all villages containing the word "wai" display evidence of a defensive wall or enclosure; and not all walled villages contain the character "wai" in their place names (for example, Ping Kong Village, near Fanling in the north-central New Territories).

There are nearly 100 New Territories village place names containing "wai", including villages which no longer exist, or are in ruins. Of these, only twenty-six villages retain full enclosing walls today, although many more retain fragments. However, "wai" also appears in many locations where there is no present-day physical evidence of enclosure, and no oral history indicating the historic existence of walls. The reason for this may be that, at some time in the last three hundred years, the character "wai" might have taken on a different meaning, implying safety rather than physical enclosure. Alternatively, the walls of many "wai"-named villages may have existed at one time, but as the threat of bandits declined, deteriorated and were eventually demolished. Only further

research, combining oral history and archaeology, can test this.

In China walled villages are found only in western Fujian Province, southern Jiangxi, and Guangdong Provinces, in the southeast coastal region of China. Walled villages are not found in the north, where protective wall enclosures or fortifications are limited to cities or territorial boundaries. The imperial courtyard house tradition of the north, with its interior orientation and spatial hierarchy, uses closed walls and gates to ensure privacy rather than defence. What accounts for the limitation of the wai to the southeast coastal region of China? One partial answer lies in the fertile nature of this region. Poor villages have little need of enclosure: they own nothing worth stealing. Conversely, wealthy agricultural villages possess both the resources to construct fortifications, and the surplus wealth, in the form of livestock and grain, requiring storage within protective walls. For this reason, the wais of the New Territories are found mostly in the flat, fertile areas, such as Kam Tin and Ping Shan.

The prevalence of walled villages in the southeast coastal region is often attributed to the presence of Japanese pirates, who regularly attacked coastal villages throughout the 16th and 17th centuries, and then to Taiwan-based rebels and outlaws, opposed to the Manchu regime, who continued to attack the coast until late in the 17th century. In 1662, the Chinese regional Viceroy and the Guangdong Governor, acting on orders form the imperial administration in Beijing, decreed the evacuation of the villages and towns of the southeast coastal plane. This policy of removal 27 kilometres (50 li) inland was intended to

choke off supplies to raiding parties of Japanese pirates and Taiwan-based Ming rebels. Farmers were not only forbidden to provision the raiders, but forced to abandon their homes and villages, resulting in starvation for many. The order was a failure, and was rescinded seven years later. To speed the recovery of the area, immigration was encouraged, and Hakka people migrated to the southeast coastal region for the first time. Unfortunately, piracy and inter-village raids proved endemic to the New Territories, and continued to inspire the construction of enclosing walls and other defensive measures among Hakka and Punti alike, well into the 19th century.

While there is some variation in the size and layout of the twenty-odd surviving walled villages of the New Territories built in the local style, with not all villages featuring corner watchtowers and moats, they are generally square or rectangular in plan, with interior row houses oriented in the same direction as the signle entrance gate. Internal lanes are quite regular, forming a comb pattern, with a single wide spinal lane running back from the entrance gate, usually to a small "god hall" or temple opposite to the gate. This central lane bisects the village, and narrow side-lanes, perpendicular to this central spine on either side, define a double comb-shaped village plan. This comb-shaped plan, with rows of houses separated by narrow lanes, is characteristic of villages throughout the Pearl River Delta. However, in Guangdong and elsewhere in the Southern coastal region, this village type is only occasionally enclosed with fortifications. Within the New Territories, this Pearl River Delta plan prevails both in walled villages and in villages without enclosures.

Many rich villages, in the bandit-ridden years of the past, surrounded themselves with strong granite walls. Normally there was only one narrow gateway and this was often protected by strong iron gates and heavy wooden doors. These iron-link gates at Ma Wat Wai are over two hundred and fifty years old.

TSANG TAI UK   RICHARD STOTT

While many villages, like Tsang Tai Uk and Lo Wai, had complete perimeter walls, others could only afford a single tower for the village guns, and as a place of refuge in the event of bandit attack. Few isolated gun towers survive in Hong Kong. The one at Hok Tau Wai is the best preserved.

LUNG YEUK TAU, LO WAI   RICHARD ABRAHALL

HOK TAU WAI   KIM APLIN

Although most walled villages include wells, livestock pens, and other necessities to see the village through a siege, some essential elements of village life were deliberately left outside the walls. No New Territories wai has an ancestral hall within its walls. There are several reasons for this. A single ancestral hall may house tablets for ancestors that are common to many branches of a lineage, resident in several villages. If ancestral halls were enclosed, residents of other villages would not freely or easily be able to fulfil their filial duty by honouring common ancestors, as the private space enclosed by the walls was not open to non-residents. Ancestral halls also serve as public ceremonial space, and are used to welcome guests, which was considered to be not quite proper within the private space enclosed by the walls. Finally, ancestral halls are designed with special geometry to allow free passage of various elements and forces to and from the ancestral altar. To enclose the ancestral tablets would be bad fung shui practice. For the same reasons, public temples, serving a whole district, are never found within the walls, although small private temples, or god-halls, open only to the residents within the walls, and communal domestic altars, were allowed within the walls, and the god-halls were often given a special position at the end of the spinal line, opposite the entrance gate, on the central axis of the village. Gatehouses themselves often contained small shrines. These gatehouses have been preserved in many villages while the enclosing walls have deteriorated or been demolished. Besides ancestral halls, other functions and structures which were never included within the New Territories wai were through roads and markets, for similar reasons: the separation of public and private spaces and functions.

Kat Hing Wai, the walled village most frequented by tourists visiting Hong Kong, typifies this Pearl River Delta village plan. This village is perfectly regular in plan, featuring a main central lane ten feet wide, flanked on both sides by identical row houses, with ten units per row, six rows per side. Narrow lanes, three feet in width, create fire separation and provide ventilation between each row and access to the houses. Although many of its interior dwelling units have been altered or rebuilt in the last thirty years, the original plan is still discernible. Storerooms, latrines, and animal sheds are located against the inner face of the periphery walls. At Kat Hing Wai, most of the dwelling units originally comprised three parts, with a front room of ten by twelve feet, a central courtyard, and a back room equal in size to the front room, featuring a cockloft reached by ladder. A few smaller units comprised only the courtyard and the back room. These units were constructed without fenestration, and relied on the front entrance and courtyard for light and ventilation. Cooking facilities were located in the courtyard. The front room was for greeting visitors, and the rear room the private family space, used for sleeping and storage. Residences at some other wais were somewhat smaller.

The enclosing walls at Kat Hing Wai mark out a rectangle 275 by 290 feet, with watch towers of twenty five feet in height at the four corners. The walls themselves are 18 feet in height, and feature gun slots near the parapets. The moat is twenty feet wide, crossed by a stone bridge. The entrance faces west, for local fung shui reasons having to do with the location of surrounding hills and water. The siting of the wai, with an open field to the front, stretching to the sea, gives a sense of openness, balanced by the presence of the Nam Tau Shan mountain range across the bay, which keeps good influences from being washed away. The hills located to the north, south, and east of the village form a sheltering "armchair", embracing and sheltering the village, and represent an optimum fung shui setting.

The history of Kat Hing Wai is similar to that of other Punti-built villages of the New Territories. The village was constructed by the Tang clan c.1465-1487, on the site of an earlier Tang village. The two neighbouring wais, Tai Hong Wai and Wing Lung Wai, were built during the same period. The enclosing walls, watchtowers, and moats of all three villages are free-standing, and were added c.1662-1721; according to local legend, to protect the inhabitants from raiding bandits and pirates. Nearby unwalled villages of later construction were built as the population expanded, exceeding the capacity of Kat Hing Wai and its two neighbours.

Wai Noi, a five-sided walled village within the larger village complex of Sheung Shui, northwest of Fanling, has a similar construction history to Kat Hing Wai. The village site was originally occupied by a Punti clan, the Kans, and taken over by the Liu family in the early Qing period. This latter family may originally have been Hakka although it has long been regarded as Punti. According to the family genealogy, the village was enclosed in 1646, to protect the family from a Ming loyalist bandit, Li Wanzong. Only a small portion of this original wall remains, measuring thirty feet in height and two feet in width. The wall was augmented by a large, shallow moat, measuring thirty to fifty feet in width, by five watchtowers, one at each corner of the wai (these are no longer standing), and by an extremely narrow entrance, barred by iron gates. The physical plan of Wai Noi follows the comb-shaped, Pearl River Delta tradition, and is quite similar to that of Kat Hing Wai: the houses of the village measure twelve feet by thirty feet, with front and back units separated by a courtyard, and with the rear units featuring cocklofts. The lanes providing fire separation, access, and ventilation between each row of houses are six feet in width. All houses are aligned with the front entrance, and oriented west-south-west, for local fung shui reasons, so that nearby hills form a sheltering ridge behind the village.

Although Wai Noi was enclosed prior to the evacuation order (1662-1668), the village fell

CORNER TOWER, KAM TIN, KAT HING WAI RICHARD ABRAHALL

BEYOND THE METROPOLIS:
VILLAGES IN HONG KONG
CHAPTER FOUR - HONG KONG'S WAI:
DEFENSIVE ARCHITECTURE OF THE NEW TERRITORIES

GUN TOWER, HOK TAU WAI   RICHARD ABRAHALL

Gun towers, whether at the corner of walled villages, or independent structures, all have a gun platform at the top, usually with small gunports for firing through. The guns used were mostly long jingals or small cannon, but few survived the confiscations of the Japanese.

within the affected area, and family tradition cites "homeless wandering with untold suffering" during the seven years the order remained in effect. The Lius were able to re-occupy their village following the rescinding of the order, but bandits continued to plague the area well into the 20th century. While the Police brought considerably greater security to the area after the takeover of the New Territories, occasional incursions of bandits from across the border kept the defences a matter of continuing vital need to the villages in this part of the New Territories right up to the end of World War Two. The wai, with its defensive walls, watchtowers and gun emplacements, continued throughout this period to play an essential role in the protection of livestock, crops, and villagers.

Further similar Punti walled villages are Tai Wai, more properly termed Chik Chuen Wai, and Tin Sam, both in Sha Tin, which were fortified in the mid-17th century in defence against the same bandit as worried the Wai Nai villagers. To construct these fortified villages, a dozen separate clans combined, consolidating a scattered group of tiny hamlets into a defensible compound. The Tai Wai villagers remember the eminent fung shui specialist hired to set out the new village site, and the unfortunate incident when, angered by jeers from some village boys, he flung down his instruments and left. Only after the elders abjectly apologised did he tell them what to do. Tai Wai is built as an approximate square, with the corner watch towers facing the cardinal points, and the entrance facing the optimum local fung shui direction; here, north-east. Within the walls, residences of the various families are not separated, but the entire community lives in mixed groups of row-houses. Both at Tai Wai and at Tin Sam, the village communities sponsored the foundation of undefended subordinate villages outside the walls when population growth exceeded the capacity of the walled enclosure. Tai Wai, Tin Sam, and also Nga Tsin Wai in Kowloon, are good examples of multi-surname walled villages: it is not correct to assume that all walled villages in the New Territories were founded or inhabited by descendants of a single clan.

The walled villages of the New Territories, with their row houses and stone or brick perimeter walls with corner towers, represent one type of regional defensive architecture, but there was a second type of village fortification practised in South China. In areas of Southern China where imperial control was weak, such as the remote and mountainous areas of north-eastern Guangdong, Hakka groups built fortified communal houses of sub-rectangular or circular form with rammed earth walls. Small, identical living units were built into the perimeter walls, facing into central courtyards. As they were built well inland, these fortifications were not in defence against pirates, but protected the Hakka from bandits and provided safety during inter-village wars. Some of these structures extant today are as much as 300 years old, but others date to the mid-19th century, built as a reaction to the chaotic times of the Taiping rebellion. These rammed-earth, self-contained, walled clan communities were not called wais, but resembled the walled villages of the southeast coastal plain in their fortress-like ability to protect whole villages, and stored crops and valuables, if necessary under siege conditions. The inclusion of interior wells, and extremely thick, defensive outer walls, up to 35 feet in height, with fenestration limited to gun slots at the lower levels, is a feature of these Hakka buildings. As Hakka people were drawn southwards, encouraged both by Qing administration policy and by the non-combative nature of the resident Punti, they brought these traditions of defensive architecture with them. Hakka migrants to the New Territories, however, did not generally construct monolithic communal residences, but normally adopted the local, or Pearl River Delta, vernacular: comb-shaped, linked blocks of identical, single-family rowhouses, arrayed along parallel lanes opening off a central spinal lane. This Pearl River Delta form prevails in most villages of the New Territories; whether Punti or Hakka; enclosed wai, or unfortified hamlet.

Clear reflections of the communal fortification traditions of the Hakka are apparent in only one or two 19th and early 20th century structures in the New Territories. The New Territories villagers had, by then, already been fortifying their villages in the local style for several centuries. One village which does appear to have been influenced by Hakka traditions of defensive architecture is Tsang Tai Uk in the Sha Tin valley. Originally known as Shan Ha Wai, Tsang Tai Uk was designed and built between 1830 and 1850 by an immigrant to the area, with massive fortifications: a very high, thick, opaque enclosing wall, and four corner watchtowers. Of grey brick with granite trim, the enclosing walls and watchtowers of Tsang Tai Uk are punctuated with small gun-slit openings. The fact that the enclosing wall comprises the outer elevation of courtyard-facing residences, and is thus an original and integral component of the village design; the height and massiveness of the enclosure; and the gun slits are design elements which recall the Hakka rammed-earth houses. Many other Hakka villages in the New Territories, however, such as Sam Tung Uk in Tsuen Wan (1786), and Sheung Yiu village (circa 1830) in north Sai Kung, lack elaborate fortifications, but rely on an inward-facing orientation, with limited or no exterior fenestration, and natural or artificially elevated sites, but with low, if any, surrounding walls, to provide enclosure and protection. This type of village might be termed semi-defended. In contrast, many of the earlier New Territories wais, constructed by the Punti, or Cantonese-speaking "local" people, were built several hundred years after the villages were first settled. Examples are, as has been noted, Kat Hing Wai in Kam Tin, but San Wai and Lo Wai, two of the five walled Tang villages of the 11 that comprise Lung Yeuk Tau, northeast of Fanling, are other cases in point.

The enclosed village was so prevalent in the New Territories from 16th century onwards, that western visitors to the region frequently noted the uneasy and belligerent society that so many fortified locations implied. One such visitor, writing about inter-clan feuding in 1875, observed:

These villages were like a garrisoned fortress, inhabited by one large family or clan, and at feud with all other surrounding villages and clans.

Reverend Krone, writing in 1858, described the prevalence of market-place robbers and pirates, as well as "internecine wars... almost always raging between some or other of the villages," finding that, "in consequence of this state of affairs, fortified places called 'Wai' have sprung up throughout the district."

Physically, wais served the purpose of defense of agricultural families against pirates and bandits. Whether built by Punti or Hakka farmers, the defensive walls enclosing and defining each wai were constructed of hard-fired grey brick, or sometimes mud brick, resting on foundations of locally quarried granite. The residences and other internal structures were constructed of the same materials, with structural framing of fir, and clay tile roofs. Punti-built wais were often supplemented with moats, as at Nai Wai, in Tuen Mun, or San Wai, in Fanling. Many of these original moats have now been filled in, for safety reasons. Entrances, with small bridges spanning the moats where necessary, were barred, and quite tiny in comparison with the mass of enclosing walls in which they were set. Wais were often built to incorporate gun turrets

and watchtowers, usually located at the four corners of the village wall. The enclosing walls are usually several brick courses in thickness, enabling a sentry to walk between gun emplacements along the top of the wall.

Walled villages were only one of several types of defensive architecture which developed in the New Territories and Southern coastal region of China in the 17th through the 19th centuries. Other, non-residential, defences included military forts, constructed at strategic coastal locations, by the Chinese imperial government of the Qing period. These forts (Hong Kong examples include the mid 17th century Fan Lau Fort, originally known as Kai Yik Kok Fort on the southern tip of Lantau; the early 19th century Tung Chung Fort on the northern coast of Lantau, opposite Chek Lap Kok; and the early 18th century Tung Lung Fort, on Tung Lung Island east of Hong Kong Island) had many features in common with Hong Kong's walled villages. The forts are rectangular in shape, built of granite blocks, with walls measuring several feet in thickness, and feature corner watch towers and gun-towers over narrow gates. All of these elements can be seen to have influenced the formal design of Hong Kong's walled villages.

In addition to walled villages and the network of coastal fortifications, there is a third type of regional defensive architecture: free-standing watchtowers. These watchtowers, or "gun-towers" (pau toi), without associated walled village enclosures, are particularly common in Guangxi and Guizhou provinces just west and northwest of Guangdong; and in Xinhui, Kaiping, and Taishan counties of Guangdong province, although they are found elsewhere in Guangdong as well. In the late 19th century, some of these free-standing watchtowers were built featuring elaborate, western-influenced architectural motifs. Free-standing watchtowers of this type are to be found in Sai Kung and Sha Tau Kok in the New

Territories, on Lantau Island, and elsewhere in the New Territories. A fine example survives at Hok Tau in Lau Shui Heung. Watchtowers are usually narrow and tall, ranging from 25 to 90 feet in height (those built in the New Territories are relatively small in comparison to the late 19th century central Guangdong watchtowers), and not normally used as residences, but for storing crops and valuables. The village guns and gunpowder were stored here, usually in a locked upper store-room, and the flat roof was provided with a parapet or screen wall to permit it to be used as a fighting platform when necessary.

A single watchtower was significantly less expensive to build than a full set of enclosing walls, but even a single tower was beyond the means of some settlements. Some smaller villages were resourceful in site design, employing natural topography and artificial earthworks to advantage, and building defensive walls only along their most exposed front, as at Sheung Yiu; or constructing fighting platforms only over the entrance gate, as at Keng Hau in Sha Tin. Krone observed that some Guangdong villages constructed small auxiliary fortress, or walled enclosures, for the defensive retreat of residents in times of attack. These enclosures were not permanent settlements, and did not include any residences. In case of attack, villagers would build temporary tented shelters. Such fortresses were small, and lacked a formal plan. There are no clear surviving examples of such walled enclosures without permanent residences in the New Territories, although oral history accounts by villagers at Shek Pik on Lantau described one such shelter, for the intermittent safekeeping of livestock, valuables, women, children, and the elderly, which was in ruins by about 1900.

Architecture alone was not sufficient to protect the agricultural villages of the New Territories from bandit raids: even the tallest of enclosures could be breached without vigilance on the part of residents. James Steward Lockhart, the Colonial Secretary assigned to survey the newly leased New Territories in 1898, found that villages typically supported from two to six constables, or kang fu. These constables, whose salaries were paid from village taxes levied on resident property owners, kept watch over village property, particularly at night, and had the power to arrest intruders. The night watch beat an hourly "all clear" signal, and patrolled the lanes within the village, and maintained a post at the entrance gateway. Some villages were equipped with a secure cell in which to detain offenders. Each family contributed to the defense of the village; if not with cash, then with labour: all the village youth were trained to defend the wai in the event of attack. An area outside the village walls was often dedicated to this martial arts training. At Tai Wai in Sha Tin, the villagers paid a martial arts teacher, giving him a free home in a watchtower and adjacent building in addition to a salary. Tai Wai village, like many other villages, also maintained a stock of spears and halberds and two small cannon, and kept an alarm gong in the entrance gate, to call villagers in from the fields whenever suspicious looking groups were seen. Tai Wai's youth militia defended not only the village property and enclosure, but provided escorts to village women going to market in an era when tigers still roamed the Lion Rock. In the eastern New Territories, village patrols were augmented by inter-village mutual defence alliances, or Yeuk, in the later 19th century. The Yeuk were empowered by their members to both arrest and sentence petty criminals.

The walled villages of the New Territories developed as part of a southeast coastal tradition of defense against pirates and bandits. The usual form of the New Territories wai is, as already noted, basically very similar to that of the Pearl River Delta and New Territories undefended villages. Some villages were founded first and fortified later: in such cases, this regular plan may have facilitated the fortification. In some of these cases a phase of semi-fortification may have preceded the full enclosure of the village. Other villages, however, included fortifications from the start, including Tai Wai and Tsang Tai Uk. The fact that walls were sometimes added after construction of the village partly explains why adjacent villages differ, with some having enclosing walls and some lacking enclosing walls. As the members of adjacent agricultural communities were likely to have kinship ties with one another, one or two fortified villages could provide a place of retreat for poorer cousins or connections in times of danger. The form of the New Territories walled village is functional and based on regional vernacular models, but it is also an expression of Chinese culture and Confucian values. The extended family, or district community, pools its resources to "develop" an agricultural site, creating both a village and a protective wall, in the one case safeguarding the perpetuation of a particular lineage group within a larger clan, or, in the other, ensuring that the community develops as a close-knit and powerful group within the wider market-town district.

In the case of Wai Noi, for instance, the construction of that walled village, divided into four equal quadrants, each quadrant occupied by the descendants of one man, provided a means of amalgamating several lineage branches of the Liu family, so that no single branch dominated the others in ritual observance or management of communal property. The geometry of the village reinforced the equitable designation of family heads eligible for election to the governing village council, under the traditional patriarchal structure. Equally, at Tai Wai, the wai, with its costituent families living mixed together, but separated from other local families by the walls, fostered the deep feeling of the villagers that all those families eligible to live there were "brothers" no matter what their surname, and that they were set apart from the other people living in the district.

The walled village itself, then, served an administrative function: providing a mechanism for equitable decision-making, removing potential strife from the ritual observances of ancestor and earth-god worship, and generally providing a framework in which the relations of family heads to each other was fixed according to Confucian principles. In the absence of a Western-style elected local governments, the village council and elders officiated at rites, ceremonies and celebrations at the village ancestral hall or temple, collected rents, and paid taxes to the central government and feudal taxlord. Finally, the council on occasion invested in the construction of satellite villages when population growth exceeded the fixed capacity of the wai. The fixed geometry of the wai helped ensure that it could not grow beyond a sustainable level, economically and administratively.

Because of its sustainable nature, many writers of the last thirty years have found the south-Chinese walled village to be an ideal model of high density town planning. Unfortunately, during the same period, many such villages have been lost through redevelopment and accompanying loss of agricultural land in both the New Territories and throughout Southern China. Even in those communities which retain, or even have restored, their enclosing walls, the interior stuctures have been demolished and replaced with modern villas in the Mediterranean mode so ubiquitous to Hong Kong. More attention should be focused on the conservation of at least the facades of the surviving original houses, allowing flexible redesign of the interiors; otherwise, one or two museums may be all that remains of this significant regional built form, the New Territories walled village.

David Lung is Reader in Architecture at the University of Hong Kong and Chairman of the Antiquities Advisory Board.

HOK TAU WAI JANET STOTT

GATEHOUSE, KAM TIN, WING LUNG WAI RICHARD ABRAHALL

KAM TIN, WING LUNG WAI, SPINAL LANE RICHARD ABRAHALL

Gatehouses of walled villages also often had gun platforms and gunports above the entrance. Inside walled villages, there is usually a central spinal lane running from the entrance back to a small temple against the back wall. The houses open off alley ways that run at right angles to this spinal lane. Most of these lanes are today cemented, but in some places, as at Wing Lung Wai, traces of the original granite slab surfaces can be seen.

CANNON, KAM TIN, KAT HING WAI RICHARD ABRAHALL

At Kat Hing Wai, one of the village cannon survives. It was not for show. In the past, in many parts of the New Territories, defence of a village from bandit attack, or from enemy villages in an inter-village war, was a very real need.

PING SHAN
[OMITTING RECENT DEVELOPMENTS]

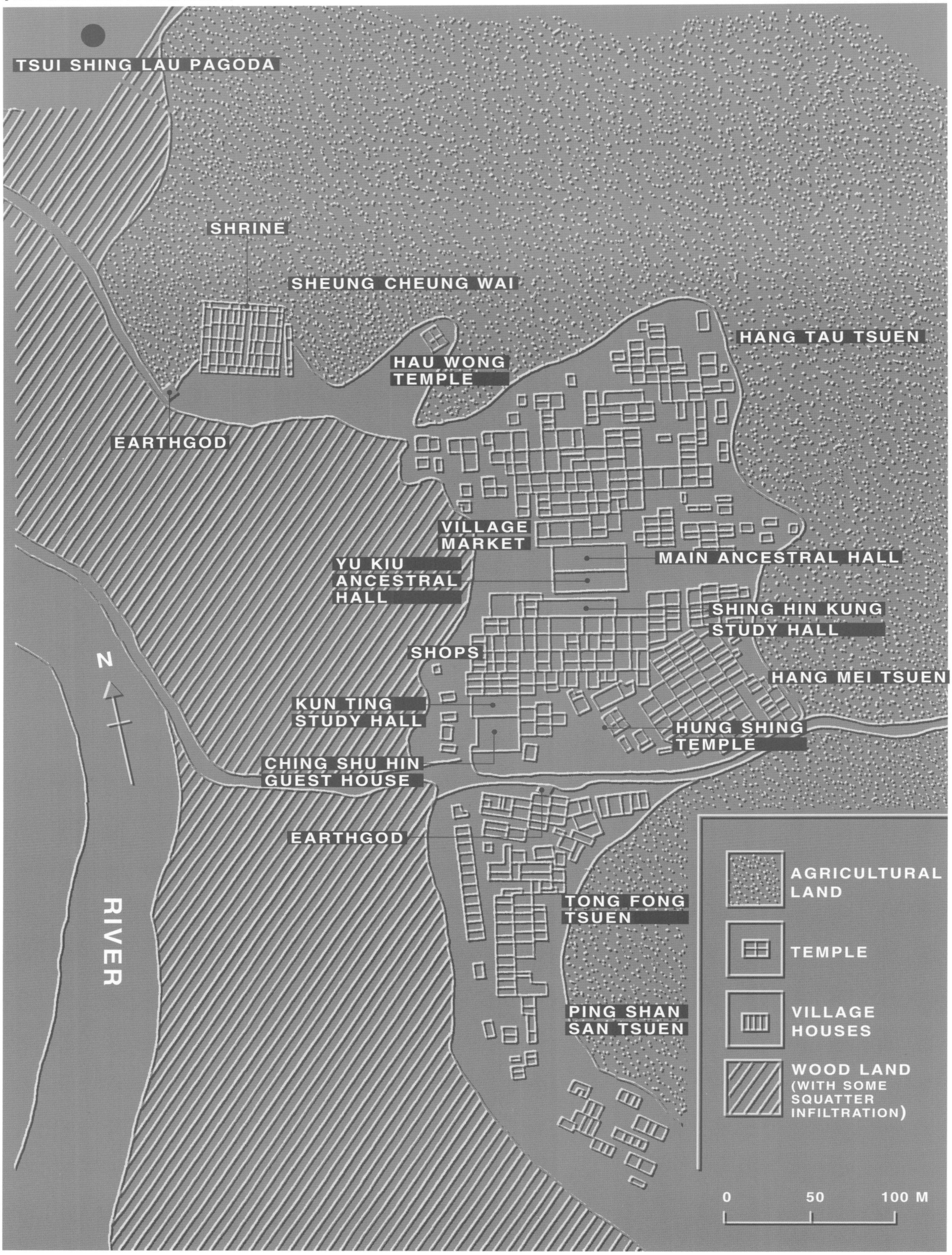

TSUI SHING LAU PAGODA

SHRINE

SHEUNG CHEUNG WAI

HANG TAU TSUEN

HAU WONG
TEMPLE

EARTHGOD

VILLAGE
MARKET

MAIN ANCESTRAL HALL

YU KIU
ANCESTRAL
HALL

SHING HIN KUNG
STUDY HALL

SHOPS

HANG MEI TSUEN

KUN TING
STUDY HALL

HUNG SHING
TEMPLE

N

CHING SHU HIN
GUEST HOUSE

RIVER

EARTHGOD

TONG FONG
TSUEN

PING SHAN
SAN TSUEN

AGRICULTURAL
LAND

TEMPLE

VILLAGE
HOUSES

WOOD LAND
(WITH SOME
SQUATTER
INFILTRATION)

0   50   100 M

CHAPTER FIVE

PING SHAN:
A GREAT CLAN VILLAGE

PING SHAN:
A GREAT CLAN VILLAGE

DAN WATERS

THE GREAT CLANS

About half the population of the New Territories when the British took over in 1898 were Hakka. The Hakka lived mostly in the more mountainous eastern and southern parts of the New Territories, where they scraped a living from often very small areas of agricultural land. Not surprisingly, it has been these poor mountainside villages which have, over the last twenty or so years, become abandoned or suffered sharp drops in population as the villagers have left to seek greener pastures in the city or overseas. The houses of such villages, with thick fung shui woods behind them, and abandoned paddy in front, surrounded by the silent hills, are very evocative and intensely picturesque. It can come as no surprise, therefore, that this book concentrates on the small, predominantly Hakka villages of the mountainous parts of the New Territories.

However, concentration on these mountainside villages can distort the historical and social picture. The first Han Chinese agricultural settlers of the area were Cantonese-speaking Punti families, and they chose to settle primarily in the rich, flat, fertile lands in the west and north of the New Territories. In the south and east they settled wherever there were broad, fertile valleys — at Sha Tin, Kowloon City, and Ho Chung, for instance. The earliest Punti clans settled in this area in the eleventh century.

Over time, the families of these early Punti settlers developed into complex, wealthy lineages. Each such lineage had a group of villages inhabited solely by lineage members, either forming a loose sprawl of settlement or scattered about, half a mile or so apart from each other. In either case, all the agricultural land within one or two miles of the villages

would be owned by members of the lineage, thus forming a home territory for the lineage, an area from which outsiders were excluded. Within the home territory, all property was owned by lineage members, and the only resident outsiders until recent times were either hereditary serfs of the lineage, or doctors, teachers, or other professionals permitted to rent houses because of the desirable skills they brought. These complex, wealthy lineages have come to be known as "the Great Clans".

Outside the home territory a Great Clan would normally have had a circle of tenant villages, economically dominated by the lineage and politically taking their leadership from the lineage. Other nearby villages, even though not tenants, were politically dominated by them and followed their leadership. Before the coming of the British, the Great Clan would keep order within its zone of influence by patrols of the clan militia, made up of young men from poorer families of the clan. The only villages which were able to keep their independence of action were medium sized Punti villages, with perhaps one or two tenant villages, which found themselves at the interstices of several Great Clan areas of influence, and could play their neighbours off against each other.

Within the mountainous east and south of the New Territories, where the arable land was not extensive enough to allow major zones of influence to develop, nonetheless the same pattern had emerged, either with clusters of small villages acknowledging the leadership of a distant major lineage, or medium size locally resident Punti clans claiming leadership over a small area of half a dozen villages.

This social pattern, with wealthy lineages dominating a zone of dependent villages, was the norm throughout the New Territories from at least the fifteenth to the nineteenth centuries.

During the nineteenth century, the villages in the mountainous east and south formed mutual defence alliances, or yeuk, and were able either to eject the Punti lineages which had dominated them previously, or at least to put the relationship onto a more equal basis. The Sha Tin and Sha Tau Kok areas may have been the first to form yeuk alliances, in the 1820s and 1830s, but the formation of yeuk continued throughout the nineteenth century. When the British came in 1898, most of the eastern and southern parts of the New Territories were within self regulating yeuk alliance districts, but most of the western and northern parts were still under the firm control of Great Clans as they had been for centuries. While the coming of the British led to changes, the Great Clans retained, in practice, much influence in these parts of the New Territories, down to World War II, or even later.

Within the dominant Punti Great Clans there were rich and poor families: a clan was powerful because of its wealth as a whole, not because it contained individual wealthy families. The power came firstly from strength in numbers — the ancient Great Clan villages usually included hundreds of families, while the individual tenant villages were typically very much smaller. Communal wealth was also important. Great clans owned many trusts held in the name of clan ancestral halls or temples, and this provided them with the communal wealth they needed.

THE TANGS

The Tangs first settled in the Hong Kong area at Kam Tin, in the mid eleventh century. During the following three centuries, branches of the clan settled at various places, both within what is now the New Territories, and further to the north, near Dongguan City. Within the

Fine walls of well-laid blue brick, and proudly curved rooflines with stucco decorations proclaim this the residence of a wealthy member of this rich clan.

New Territories, the Tangs established themselves at Ping Shan, Ha Tsuen, Lung Yeuk Tau, Tai Po Tau, and Loi Tung, as well as at Kam Tin. In each place the Tangs became the dominant lineage of the area. With this number of home territories the Tangs became the most powerful of the "Five Great Clans" of the New Territories. This was especially so in the Yuen Long Plain, with Ha Tsuen, Kam Tin, and Ping Shan sharing most of the area between them.

The influence of the Tangs would have been overwhelming had it not been that the various branches were usually at enmity between themselves. Ping Shan was thus usually at enmity with Ha Tsuen over the ownership of the important ferry over the Hung Shui Kiu River, and had never forgiven Kam Tin for having wrested control of the Yuen Long Market from Ping Shan, and for moving it physically from the Ping Shan to the Kam Tin bank of the Yuen Long River, in the later seventeenth century.

PING SHAN

Ping Shan was, from the late fourteenth century until the coming of the British, a Great Clan village cluster controlling the land south of the Yuen Long River as far as the Hung Shui Kiu River. Its wealth and power were shown by possession of impressive ancestral halls and other communal buildings, using the best possible materials, which, by their grave magnificence, dominated the view of any traveller passing by. These impressive buildings were designed to make a clear political statement — it was only a Great Clan which could erect such buildings, and they put the tiny single-roomed ancestral halls of the tenant villages firmly into their place. Many of these impressive communal buildings have survived at Ping Shan, and have recently been restored with Government assistance, to form a "Heritage Trail". Ping Shan remains fully inhabited, and most of its traditional houses have been rebuilt into more comfortable modern places, but its ancient communal buildings remain to give the visitor a real flavour of Great Clan pride, power, wealth, and history.

Ping Shan consists of a sprawl of buildings, with the five villages of the clan almost indistinguishably merging into one another along the western face of the low fung shui hill which gives the place its name ("Screen Hill"). The village sits astride the road from Yuen Long to the coast at Sha Kong Miu near Lau Fau Shan. In the past this road was more important than today, as it carried the traffic from the County City at Nantou to Kowloon City via a ferry which went across Deep Bay to Sha Kong Miu.

The village square at Ping Shan, a little to the north of the main road, separates the two largest villages, Hang Mei ("Tail of the Stream") and Hang Tau ("Head of the Stream"), although the stream has long since been replaced by a small concrete nullah. This square, in front of the ancestral halls, with its early morning market and children at play, has for generations been the centre of community life for the members of the clan. In front of the square, guarded by an antique cannon, representing the military strength of the clan, some of the finest rice in Hong Kong used to grow. Around the square used to stand the largest and best built of the old-style village houses. Few remain, although one or two still delight the eye with their sweeping gables.

A little to the north-west of the village square stands the Sheung Cheung Wai Walled Village, built originally with grey-green bricks, probably in the 18th century. It has a heavy granite plinth and lookout windows higher up. Originally, its walls were otherwise not pierced by openings, except for the single entrance gate and gunslits at appropriate locations. Its walls offered protection to the whole clan against bandits, pirates and other marauding clans.

The remains of an old-fashioned "drawn door", made up of timber poles at intervals so that ventilation is not restricted, is all that is left of the gate of Sheung Cheung Wai itself. Spiritual protection is provided by the "Five Happiness" (long life, wealth, health, virtue, and a natural death), five pieces of gold speckled red paper hanging up just inside the entrance to the walled village, above a small shrine. The design of this walled village is the standard one traditional in the New Territories, with a single spinal line running from the gate back to a shrine, and narrow access lanes opening off on either side to the houses.

In order to arrive at "harmony and balance" between heaven, earth and man, and prevent "chi", the spirit of vitality of fung shui, from being swept away by the stream that used to flow in front of this hamlet and out to Deep Bay, this walled village faces directly south. This is the optimum "Red-bird" (fung shui) aspect in this location. In the New Territories the optimum fung shui direction is only occasionally south. By demonstrating faith in the powers of nature villagers ensure their good fortune.

Forty years ago most of the houses, especially in Hang Tau and Hang Mei villages, were built in traditional style, and most were in reasonable condition, although a few were already falling into disrepair. Most of these houses were well-built, of brick, often with painted or stucco eaves decoration. Since then, many of the traditional structures have been torn down to make way for more commodious and comfortable places.

The hovels at the rear of the villages are a different story. They are where the "ha foo" ("sai man") once lived. These hereditary servants ministered to the needs of the Clan. Children purchased from poor families became general dogsbodies. After coming of age they were married off, but any offspring became serfs too, like their mothers and fathers, and belonged to their owners. The custom died a natural death during the Second World War.

Every village of any size had a school: rich villages, like Ping Shan, had several. Sitting at small wooden desks, the village boys would spend many hours memorising the Four Books from ill-printed copies, and learning the rules of polite behaviour and virtuous conduct.

PING SHAN, MAIN ANCESTRAL HALL KIM APLIN

The centre of clan life is the Ancestral Hall. In single-clan villages like Ping Shan it is also the centre of village life. In most villages it is the best-built and most lavishly finished building, the degree of expense spared on it a clear indication of the wealth of the clan. At Ping Shan, the fine granite pillars, steps, and courtyards proclaim a highly prestigious clan. In this Hall clan and village feasts are held, and funerals conducted. Here the elders great high-ranking guests. Meetings of the elders are held here, and the village office occupies a side-room. Honour-boards recognise those of the clan who have brought honour and fame to the clan. Hanging high on a wall is the character "Filial Piety", as a perpetual reminder to the youngsters of the clan being taught in one of the village schools, such as the nearby Kun Ting Study Hall.

PING SHAN, MAIN ANCESTRAL HALL KIM APLIN

PING SHAN, HONOUR BOARD IN MAIN ANCESTRAL HALL KIM APLIN

PING SHAN, KUN TING STUDY HALL, ENTRANCE KIM APLIN

Previously, they were the only permanent inhabitants of these villages not surnamed Tang.

THE ANCESTRAL HALLS

One of the ways a Great Clan made a public statement of its dominant position within its district was by building grand and impressive ancestral halls. Chinese imperial law permitted self-standing ancestral halls with two or more courts, and flights of steps leading from court to court, only to clans which had achieved high imperial honours. Other clans had to make do with just a single room in a row of buildings. Within the New Territories, possession of a self-standing ancestral hall is the mark of a Great Clan. Such a hall is a statement of the clan's antiquity, of its origins from a high imperial official, and its continuing commitment to learning. There can be no doubt that such grand ancestral halls did achieve their aim of overawing the tenants and dependants of the clan.

In the village square outside the Ping Shan ancestral halls are half-a-dozen pairs of granite flag-staff stands erected to commemorate high successes in the imperial examinations by members of the clan. The clan had the right to raise such a flag-staff for each successful candidate, with a banner detailing the success. Every passer-by, and especially every non-Tang, had to bow before the banners. With the ancestral halls standing fronting the market, these flag-staffs were a perpetual reminder to the clan tenants and dependants of the high status of the clan. Even now, after the flag-staffs have long rotted away, the Tangs are proud of the fame brought them by their long-dead ancestors. The granite stands are carefully preserved. Eminent scholars brought honour and glory to the clan. Success in the imperial examinations meant exemption from taxes, and corvee for candidates and family members, and legal and political privileges, as well as political leverage in the district.

There are two large ancestral halls opening off the market square at Ping Shan. Both have recently been beautifully restored. The more northern of the two is slightly the larger, and has a slightly higher roof line, although neither of these features is immediately apparent at first glance. This hall is the main hall, which holds the ancestral tablet of the founding ancestor of the Ping Shan branch of the Tangs. It was originally built by a fifth generation descendant, Tang Fung-shun, probably in the early sixteenth century, although the present building is early eighteenth century. The adjacent hall, the Yu Kiu Ancestral Hall was built in the early eighteenth century by two 17th generation descendants, the brothers Tang Sai-yin (alias Yu-sing) and Tang Sai-chu (alias Kiu-lum) to commemorate their father and his descendants.

Digging the foundations for the Tang ancestral halls would have started on a propitious day. A second special occasion would have been setting the main door in position. This would have been decorated with a piece of red paper on which was written, "Door of Peace and Good Fortune". But the most important ceremony, witnessed by the entire male community of the village, would have been hoisting the ridge-poles draped with such objects as small bags of grain, a paper lantern and a pair of trousers, signifying important acquisitions like sons and wealth. For the communal buildings of a Great Clan, like the Ping Shan Tangs, every stage in construction would have been conducted with lavish public ritual and ceremonial designed to reinforce the clan's public position and status.

The Ping Shan ancestral halls share a common plan. Each has a deep roofed entrance hall open to the village square, with the roof held up by granite pillars cut from single blocks of stone, and wooden beams and brackets of the intensely hard kwan-din wood. The beams and brackets are exquisitely carved, to standards the equal even of the great public buildings in Canton. Under the eaves are broad bands of fine eaves paintings. Below this, the walls are of severe and unrelieved polished blue brick, most carefully laid, with granite plinths. Special decorative features include ceramic unicorns and grotesque dragon fish, which decorate the ridge-lines, and stucco work on some eaves finishes.

On either side of the doors are drum platforms, filing the entrance hall, except for the stone-paved entrance way to the doors. This entrance way is paved with blood-red sandstone imported at great expense from near Canton: this stone is used also inside the hall to define the main processional way across the courtyard. The drum platforms, of granite, and about three-feet high, were used for musicians who would play to add grandeur to high clan rituals. At other times, Tang clan elders would sit here to adjudicate disputes, or to preside over mass meetings of the residents in the square.

Behind the drum platforms are the great doors, well over twice the height of a man, massive and heavy, and painted dark red with fine examples of the protective door-gods.

Inside the main doors there is a deep porch, with storerooms for clan communal possessions, including various ritual vessels, and the furniture and crockery for clan feasts, on either side. These open into a large courtyard, which is used for the initial stages of certain major rituals.

At the opposite side of this courtyard is a hall, open to the courtyard, with the roof again held up with fine granite pillars and exquisitely carved kwan-din beams and brackets. This hall is about four feet higher than the courtyard. This hall was and still is used for clan feasts, and as the meeting hall of the clan elders: it was also used for funerals of the elders. The Yu Kiu ancestral hall housed the Tat Tak Primary School until 1961: and the first courtyard hall was used by the school when not required for clan purposes. The first courtyard hall in the main ancestral hall was used, when not required for clan purposes, for the martial arts training of the clan militia. On the side walls of these halls hang honour boards recording examination successes or other honours awarded to clansmen.

Two entrances, at the back, lead from the first courtyard hall, into the smaller second courtyard. From here, further flights of steps reach up to another raised platform. Here, behind a screen, is the great ancestral altar, with its racks of ancestral tablets picked out in gold, rising up in eight rows to the tablet of the founding ancestor high above the floor. These tablets measure about 9 inches by 2 inches. The names and other details of the ancestor and his wife are carved on the front. Many, particularly the tablets of those who achieved high imperial honour, are made of two pieces of wood slotted together, allowing an ink-written further biography to be added to the inner surfaces. These biographies and other details form the core of the clan genealogy, kept for the whole lineage by the elders.

In many Great Clan ancestral halls there are three ancestral altars; a central one to the high clan ancestors, a side altar to those ancestors who donated significantly to the building or repair of the hall, and another, on the other side, to ancestors who have brought honour to the clan. But the Ping Shan halls have only the altar to the high clan ancestors. In the main ancestral hall, the areas alongside the main ancestral altar were used as offices for the clan militia (nowadays, these are used as the village office), and, in the Yu Kiu hall, as offices for the school.

In the main ancestral hall, two huge (six foot high) characters ("filial piety", "brotherly love") hang on the side-walls beside the ancestral altar to remind all clansmen of the virtues the ancestral hall stands for, and to reinforce the need for clan solidarity and unity essential to maintaining their position as a Great Clan.

In addition to the two large ancestral halls in the village square, other segments of the clan maintain other ancestral halls elsewhere in the village. There is one near the north-eastern corner of Hang Tau village, for instance, as well as altars within the private study halls, for the descendants of the founders.

The Ping Shan ancestral halls are still used for Clan rituals, where the living, in the presence of the dead, headed by Tang Clan elders in ceremonial robes, working down in groups, generation by generation, to the youngest boys, kowtow before the soul tablets.

With camaraderie and food playing important and symbolic roles in Chinese culture, it is not surprising that the ancestral halls are also regularly used for clan feasts. These often follow traditional "basin feast" form. Large numbers of circular tables are set out, on each of which is placed a two-foot diameter wash-hand basin. This contains the succulent roast pork which has previously been offered up before the ancestors. There is also layer upon layer of other foodstuff, such as chicken, deep-fried eel, prawns, gourds, bean curd, turnips, and so on.

These great halls are most impressive. In their severe beauty, especially following the recent highly sensitive restoration, they express Great Clan power and pride very clearly, and reflect, even to the present, Great Clan unity and self-confidence.

EARTH-GODS

While worship of the ancestors was, for members of a Great Clan, the most important ritual activity, it would have been dangerous for any villager to have ignored the spirits and deities and the other myriad inhabitants of the other world. Ping Shan has the required provision for this, with a number of earth-god shrines, and two temples, but it is noticeable how much smaller, less centrally located, and less elaborately built the temples are when compared with the ancestral halls. This difference can be seen in a number of other Great Clan villages. These temples protected the village, but brought little political status or opportunity for Great Clan display.

To provide basic spiritual protection, Ping Shan has, in addition to the large earth-god shrines with decorative wing-walls which stand at each end of the villages, a number of other earth-god shrines each worshipped by defined sections of the community, or by different groups of families. The earth-god presides over the fertility of the soil and keeps a protecting eye on the residents of the area. Some of these sectional earth-gods boast little stone shrines but others are believed to reside in boulders or great trees, particularly if they have strange or unusual shapes.

On the opposite side of the road from the Hung Shing Temple, for instance, stands a grotesque, whiskery, small-leaf Chinese banyan, which is the abode of one of Ping Shan's earth gods. Alongside the tree, in front of a stone which signifies the presence of the god, a trough serves as an incense burner. Wood is one of the "Five Elements" and is the symbol of fertility and living strength. It is not unexpected, therefore, that such trees as the multi-stemmed banyan should be regarded as the residence of the god of fertility. In folk religion banyans, especially those associated with earth gods, are themselves the focus of various rituals, particularly at weddings, and for beseeching good health.

TEMPLES

In the New Territories most villages or village clusters have one or more temples. Ping Shan has two, the Yeung Hau Wong and the Hung Shing temples, both of which play significant roles in local life. The Hung Shing temple, not far from the entrance to Hang Mei village, was probably first constructed between 1764 and 1767, when tides which could wash away fields and fortunes came closer than now across the low-lying land between the village and the open sea. Ping Shan was always at risk

PING SHAN, ANCESTRAL ALTAR, MAIN ANCESTRAL HALL   KIM APLIN

On the Ancestral Altar, the tablets to the High Ancestors of the clan are displayed in rows, the Founding Ancestors at the top. The tablets are framed in elaborately carved and painted panels of woodwork. At various places around the village are earth-god shrines: some elaborate and large, some simple and small. A "dragon's head" carving probably reflects the crocodiles which used to infest the marshy waters near Ping Shan.

PING SHAN, EARTHGOD SHRINE   RICHARD STOTT

PING SHAN, KUN TING STUDY HALL, EARTHGOD SHRINE   KIM APLIN

PING SHAN   RICHARD STOTT

from typhoon-driven storm surges over-topping sea defences, and a temple to the deity with the power to control wind and wave was a valuable defence for the whole clan. Inscriptions within the temple detail the villagers' gratitude to the god for his protection: "His favours are like the sunshine illuminating the earth": "His virtues are showered like a flood on the inhabitants of the world".

The second temple, the straight-roofed Hau Wong Temple, stands between Hang Tau and Sheung Cheung Wai villages, surrounded by fung shui woods. Nearby there is an ancient well with fine stone steening. This temple was probably established in 1711, the date of the bell. In accordance with the eclecticism of traditional folk religion this temple contains an earth-god shrine in the right-hand chamber, while Kam Fa, the patron saint of expectant mothers, is housed on the left-hand side. The god, Yeung Hau Wong, who in life was supposed to have been the marquis who saved the life of the Sung Emperor, is seated in the centre.

THE PAGODA

As a further precaution, to fend off evil fung shui influences, the Tsui Shing Lau "Tower of Gathering Stars", Hong Kong's only ancient pagoda, now dwarfed by the massive, 30-odd storey blocks of flats of the adjacent Tin Shui Wai New Town, was built in alignment with Castle Peak to guard the village from a poor fung shui aspect from the north and west. Although traditionally Buddhist, most Chinese pagodas were built to improve fung shui. Tsui Shing Lau is built to a hexagonal plan, with three (possibly originally five) floors of local bricks. It has heavy granite details.

There are no records, but some villagers claim this pagoda even dates back over 600 years, to the first foundation of the village, during which time it has been damaged by typhoon and fire. If really so ancient, it would

be Hong Kong's oldest structure. It has now been beautifully restored. The 30-foot high pagoda has three propitiously named floors: "Over the Milky Way", "Pagoda of Gathering Stars" and "Light shines straight on to the Dipper". The Pagoda is dedicated to the God of Literature, who helped Tang Clan scholars of all ages attain distinction. A statue of Fui Shing, a deity controlling success in examinations, is housed here, as were, at one time, some soul tablets.

STUDY HALLS

No Great Clan could expect to maintain its dominant position unless it had a reputation for scholarship. Such a reputation of itself would have given a Great Clan considerable status and authority within its district. More importantly perhaps, a steady trickle of graduates in the imperial examinations would have kept the clan in close and amicable contact with the Magistrate. Residents in the smaller dependent villages only began, in practice, to take part in the Imperial examinations (in very small numbers) during the later nineteenth century (the local Hakka, indeed, were legally debarred from entering the examinations until the 1820s). Thus the monopoly of graduate, gentry status by the scholars of the Great Clan was an important factor in maintaining the clan's status. Not surprisingly, therefore, Ping Shan, like so many Great Clan villages, retains many buildings designed to educate clansmen.

In Ping Shan, primary schooling was traditionally provided in the Yu Kiu ancestral hall. After a basic education had been received there, further education needed a tutor. A number of study halls, designed for a tutor and a handful of pupils, survive in Ping Shan. The largest is the Shing Hin Kung Study Hall, built next to the ancestral halls, and almost as big. This was the main clan study hall, and was maintained by the clan communal trusts. The other three study halls were founded by

individuals, who set up trusts to run and maintain them. All this was an investment in the clan's future.

The Shing Hin Kung Study Hall is entered through an outer courtyard, and then through a gateway into a large inner courtyard. At the further end, up a flight of steps, there is an ancestral altar. This holds the ancestral tablets of those who paid for the building and the contemporary rebuilding of the ancestral halls. On either side are teaching rooms and residential accommodation for the tutor and any students who wished to board with him. At the time of writing this study hall, where the soul tablets have been removed from the altar, is delapidated and used as a workshop. Nonetheless, the fine brickwork and decorative finish of the building show that it was only slightly less well constructed than the ancestral halls. It is hoped it will soon be restored, so that, as originally designed, it may once again, together with the ancestral halls, form part of a combined elegant backing to the village square.

The most impressive of the other surviving study halls is named after Tang Kun-ting, one of the 21st generation of Ping Shan Tangs. Completed in 1870, the Kun Ting Study Hall also serves, with its finely carved altar and gold-lettered ancestral tablet of Tang Kun-ting, for ancestral worship of him and his immediate family. The power and wealth of the Tang Clan was at its peak when this hall was built. It is a particularly handsome and rich building. The Guangzhou and Foshan craftsmen who, together with Hong Kong masons, built it, did a masterly job. The building consists of a courtyard with teaching rooms around it, and Tang Kun-ting's ancestral altar opposite the entrance. Residential accommodation for the tutor is on either side of the ancestral altar, together with a small room screened off with a fine painted and carved screen from the courtyard. This was designed as a meeting room for the elders of Tang Kun-ting's descendants. It is still used for this purpose.

The workmanship, including plaster mouldings, clusters of brackets, lattice screen panels, wall paintings and other features, in both monochrome and polychrome, sometimes displaying the Middle Eastern or Western influences common in the region at the time, are exquisite. Cross currents of Chinese and Western cultural influences have left indelible marks on Hong Kong life which should be preserved as part of its heritage. The Chinese have a natural instinct for colour and parts of the interior of the hall are lavishly decorated with animals, birds and flowers. Peaches and plums symbolise assiduous scholarship.

The restoration of this study hall was awarded the Hong Kong Institute of Architects President's prize in 1991, as well as the 1994 Gold Medal in the category of conservation by the Architects' Regional Council of Asia. The work was executed in as authentic a way as possible. Instead of nails, bamboo pins were used to fasten timbers. Pins were "fried" to shrink them and rid them of possible termites.

Of the other study halls, the Yeuk Hoi Study Hall (next to the Hung Shing Temple), has been modernised for use as an ancestral hall for the descent line of the founder. Of the Shut Hing Study Hall in Tong Fong village, only the facade still survives.

In the Ping Shan study halls, upwards of twenty villagers studied who later became senior government officials, according to present day village elders. Others became wealthy merchants. Their education was of the old, traditional kind. Stress was on the memorising of the *Four Books* and *Five Classics*, composing couplets and essays, and preparing students to fill posts in the imperial administration. Desks and stools were uncomfortable, and corporal punishment always assisted the laggard or the slow. "To rear without teaching is a fault in the father: to teach without severity is a fault in the teacher."

Respect for learning ran deep in traditional China. Ping Shan has a long tradition of scholarship. Tang scholars from Ping Shan were frequently successful in the imperial examinations. The Shing Hin Kung study hall retains a tablet recording an achievement in 1804. Thirteen members of the clan with academic honours (including two "Kui Yan" degree holders) donated to the 1866 rebuilding of the Hung Shing temple. The presence of so many graduates in their formal robes at clan ceremonies, and when the elders greeted important visitors, must have brought great honour and authority to the clan, and these ancient schools tell us a great deal about the aspirations and public life of a Great Clan.

THE CHING SHU HIN GUESTHOUSE

A decorative gateway connects the Kun Ting Study Hall and the richly embellished Ching Shu Hin Guest House, both built about 1870. The latter resembles the elegant residence of a well-off family. In the decorative scheme for the guest house the red and yellow carp, symbol of success through endeavour, is prominent.

The villagers decided to build this guest house to provide visitors travelling through the village from the ferry pier at Sha Kong Miu with more comfortable quarters than the cocklofts in the ancestral halls. Some believe Sun Yat-sen stayed here before the 1911 Revolution. The guest house contained all that a distinguished scholar might need, including a fine kitchen, a reception room to meet other visitors and the elders, and a study on an upper floor overlooking the mountains. There is an elegant little courtyard garden entered through a moon-gate, with stands for flowerpots, ideal for sitting in to compose poetry.

This Guesthouse, which was built and maintained by the clan communally, is another physical reflection of the clan's desire to maintain its status as the dominant force in local life. Yuen Long Market had inns for visitors, run, in some cases, by Ping Shan tenants and dependants. Other lodging houses were available in the poor villages near the ferry piers. By building this extremely luxurious and comfortable guesthouse, for use, however, by prestigious visitors only, the village aimed at ensuring that such guests, as they passed through the area met only Tangs, and were insulated from contact with the Tang tenants and dependants.

CONCLUSION

Today, many of the fine buildings surviving in Ping Shan have been beautifully restored. The policy has been "minimal intervention". As far as possible traditional skills and original materials, retaining a patina of age, have been employed. This often meant searching for abandoned old structures locally, or in China, from where much of the original materials came centuries ago.

Now, these old Tang Clan buildings at Ping Shan form part of a one-kilometre long Heritage Trail. The landscape of rolling hills, peaceful fung shui woodlands and ancient, well-kept buildings, in the New Territories and over the border in southern China, is changing repidly. It is important that people pay frequent visits to places such as Ping Shan, especially the young, to remind them of their ancient culture and to increase their understanding of heritage preservation.

By visiting Ping Shan and its finely restored buildings it is easy to get a feel of what life was like in the centre of an ancient, proud, wealthy and self-confident Great Clan. Much of Hong Kong's history revolves around such clans, and the Heritage Trail, by giving to modern Hong Kong residents a taste of that history, is a most important development.

Dr. Dan D. Waters, is a Council member of the RAS and a member of the Antiquities Advisory Board. He has been in Hong Kong for over 40 years and is active in the community in many ways. He has published on various subjects. His latest book is *Faces of Hong Kong*.

Only the most prestigious buildings could afford to have finely carved iron-wood beams like this to hold up the roof, carved with auspicious symbols. Their weight, hardness, strength and resistance to damp and termites made such beams greatly prized and very expensive.

PING SHAN, CLAN GUESTHOUSE KIM APLIN

Painted and carved stucco work was a local speciality, found in both wealthy villages like Ping Shan, and in less prestigious places like Hok Tau Wai. Much of this work is now damaged by rain and storm, but these restored examples from Ping Shan show how exquisite this work was when new. Filgree panels, preserving privacy, but allowing air to pass are another elegant local speciality. as are painted, carred and stuio-work decorations for important doors and gates.

PING SHAN, CLAN GUESTHOUSE KIM APLIN

HOK TAU WAI RICHARD STOTT

PING SHAN, CLAN GUESTHOUSE JANET STOTT

PING SHAN, ENTRANCE TO CLAN GUESTHOUSE RICHARD STOTT

PING SHAN, CLAN GUESTHOUSE   JANET STOTT

PING SHAN, MAIN ANCESTRAL HALL   KIM APLIN

Moon doors are difficult to build, and expensive. These examples are in the main Ancestral Hall at Ping Shan, and the clan guest-house there, where this striking entrance marks the junction of the entrance passage and the small garden-court.

PING SHAN, KUN TING STUDY HALL   KIM APLIN

These elaborately carved and painted folding screen-doors partition off one of the teaching areas at the Kun Ting Study Hall in Ping Shan.

Beyond the
Metropolis
$60.00

*The Shing Hin Kung Study Hall, once the pride of Ping Shan, now stands rotting and full of cast-off
waste. The children of Ping Shan have been educated in modern schools for more than thirty years,
and this fine old building has been of little use. Hopefully, it can be restored soon, like its neighbour, the
Kun Ting Study Hall.*

Few of the elegant old roofs with curved wok-yee ends still survive. The homes they sheltered were satisfying to the eye, but damp and comfortless: most have been pulled door to provide space for less aesthetically satisfying, but more comfortable modern three-storey houses like those in the background.

PING SHAN   KIM APLIN

Ping Shan still has families with wealth to grace their rooms with the furniture, calligraphy, and paintings of a cultured Chinese life.

TRADITIONAL VILLAGE POLITICS:
LAU SHUI HEUNG

P.H. HASE

There is an instinctive feeling among most city-dwellers that traditional rural life was simple and unsophisticated, and that the villagers of the New Territories used to live a peaceful and bucolic existence, far removed from the political stresses and problems of the city. Nothing could be further from the truth, as even a brief look at the history of the Lau Shui Heung area shows.

The Lau Shui Heung area is in the northern New Territories, just east of Lung Yeuk Tau, and consists of a number of narrow, albeit fertile valleys. Nowhere in the area is more than a quarter of a mile from the foot of the hills, and the steep, tree-covered slopes dominate the area in every direction.

The area has had a turbulent and complex history. From the seventeenth century up to the coming of the British, the area was dominated by a small number of rich and powerful Punti clans. The Chinese imperial bureaucracy was extremely feeble in this area in the nineteenth century, and took little if any steps to control it, or to enforce order there. The area was left almost entirely to itself, so long as the imperial taxes were paid: in these circumstances, the more powerful local groups were able to monopolise local power.

All the great clans sought to dominate and control the smaller villages around them. These great clans were normally at enmity with the other great clans whose areas of influence were contiguous with theirs. If a great clan had a zone of thoroughly subordinate villages behind it, it would not have to worry about defending its rear. The more tenants and clients a great clan had, therefore, the greater its position, influence, and potential military strength. The

great clans traditionally demanded obedience from their tenants, even military support if need be. Other villages, not actually tenants of the great clan, could often be cowed into surrendering independence of action in return for protection against third parties provided by the great clan and its militia. Ties of protection could switch from great clan to great clan as part of the spoils of inter-village war or other local political developments, when it became clear that the militia patrols of the previously dominant clan were no longer able to protect the area effectively.

Few of the smaller villages relished this client status. Many of them had been founded by immigrant groups after the Coastal Evacuation of the later seventeenth century, and their tiny populations and poverty made independent action an impossibility for most of the eighteenth century. However, populations rose, and the villages became more prosperous. From the end of the eighteenth century, the smaller villages in some parts of the area were forming yeuk, or sworn mutual defence alliances, to defend themselves against the great clans, and against bandits or other threats. Such yeuk areas aimed to throw out, or at least to lessen, great clan influence, and to replace great clan militia patrols with patrols of their own, and to allow the oath-sworn villages a more independent voice in local politics and a more independent status in inter-village disputes and wars.

Thus the Sha Tau Kok area, immediately east of Lau Shui Heung, achieved independence at the latest by about 1835: this area became known as the Shap Yeuk ("The Alliance of Ten"). Independence may have been achieved

when the great clan which had previously dominated the area (the Cheungs of Wangbeiling) were too involved in one of their wars with the other great clans of the Wangbeiling area to respond to the threat from their previous clients. The Ta Kwu Leng area (the Luk Yeuk, "The Alliance of Six"), immediately to the north of Lau Shui Heung, achieved its independence in the 1860s, after a bruising war with the Cheungs of Wangbeiling. However, Ta Kwu Leng had to pay for its independence with several decades of military alertness, since Wangbeiling refused to accept their defeat as final: the very name of Ta Kwu Leng ("Drum-beat Ridge") is a memory of this troubled mid-nineteenth century period.

The Tai Po area, just to the south of Lau Shui Heung, was originally dominated by the Tangs of Tai Po Tau. This clan owned the local market at Tai Po, and made all non-Tangs sell goods at a discount to the Tangs, and to pay a toll before selling in the market. The other villages had long wanted to break this Tang monopoly, but the Tai Po Tau Tangs were strongly supported by their lineage cousins at Lung Yeuk Tau and Loi Tung, and were able to defeat the several attempts at independence by the small villages of the area between the 1840s and the 1890s. However, in 1896, the non-Tangs of the area succeeded in their main aim, and established a market of their own, and built a bridge across the line of the ferry which had previously been owned by the Tangs. The Tai Po non-Tang villages united into the Tsat Yeuk (the "Alliance of Seven") to achieve this. Because of the long-term enmity between them and the Tangs of Lung Yeuk Tau, the powerful

"Stick No Bills", but this lamp-post stands at an awkward fung shui site, so adjacent walls are placarded: "Great Good Fortune"!

clan of the Pangs of Fan Ling enthusiastically supported the Tsat Yeuk, swore the Yeuk oath with the Tai Po small villages, and took one of the seven shares in the new market, seeing this as an ideal way to cause pain and vexation to their loathed neighbours in Lung Yeuk Tau.

The tragic tale of Tang Yung-keng typifies the jealousies and enmities of the area in the mid-nineteenth century. He was a villager of Lung Yeuk Tau, and a fine scholar. He graduated as a "Tsun Sz", the highest level of the imperial examination system - one of only two or three New Territories villagers ever to achieve this high status. According to tradition, the family of the graduate would take him round all the local villages so that everyone could congratulate him. The Tangs decided to do this, finishing up in a blaze of publicity with the Pangs at Fan Ling. The Tangs were well aware that this would be to heap coals of fire on the heads of their neighbours. The Pangs, jealous to the point of suffocation at the Tang success, invited the party to a congratulatory dinner, as required by tradition. Unfortunately, Tang Yung-keng died that very night, the victim, as the Tangs believe, of poison put into the wine given him for the toast by the Pangs. This incident occurred in the late 1860s.

The thirteen or fourteen villages of Lau Shui Heung were thus founded and developed within a politically delicate area. In the Ming period there were probably six villages in the area: Lung Yeuk Tau and Loi Tung, Hung Leng, Tan Chuk Hang, Man Uk Pin, and probably Kwan Tei. Lung Yeuk Tau and Loi Tung were Tang strongholds from the early fourteenth century. Hung Leng was at that date a Hau stronghold: the Haus of Hung Leng were probably also regarded as a major clan at that date, in alliance with their lineage cousins in Ho Sheung Heung, Kam Tsin, and Ping Kong. Man Uk Pin ("The Houses of the Man Clan")

must have been a centre of the Man clan, who otherwise are to be found in Ta Kwu Leng: they were never a major clan, and must have been subordinate to one or other of the major groups in the area. Tan Chuk Hang and Kwan Tei were certainly subordinate to the major clans - each of these villages consisted of a number of very small clans, who were probably originally tenants of the nearby major lineages.

The major developments in this area during the eighteenth century were the decline of the Haus, and the extension of the cultivated area right up to the foot of the mountains. The Haus lost the support of their lineage cousins once Ho Sheung Heung and Kam Tsin in particular had lost much of their influence to the Lius of Sheung Shui, probably somewhen in the late eighteenth century. Without the support of Ho Sheung Heung and Ping Kong, the Hung Leng Haus could not withstand the pressure from Lung Yeuk Tau and Loi Tung between whom they were squeezed. The Haus of Ho Sheung Heung, the Lius, the Pangs, and the Tangs, with the Mans of San Tin and Tai Hang (a different surname from the Mans of Man Uk Pin), formed, probably in the early nineteenth century, a joint association around the Po Tak Temple in Sheung Shui, to provide for matters of common interest to the great clans: the Haus of Hung Leng were not given a share in this association, since they were already by then too insignificant to be counted as a great clan. By that date the Haus were regarded as having much the same status as their erstwhile clients at Tan Chuk Hang.

From the early eighteenth century the long settled clans of this area had to face the problem of dealing with immigrant groups. There were then many such groups coming into the area looking for undeveloped land to take up. Many areas at the head of the Lau Shui Heung valleys were in fact still undeveloped and covered with

forest in this period, and so were available for conversion to arable. The long-settled clans reacted to this situation by taking up as much land as possible themselves, to ensure that it was occupied against the possible needs of future generations, and to reduce to the minimum the areas available to newcomers. At the same time, by restricting access to undeveloped lands, the older clans were able to ensure that incoming groups remained a minority, and thus could be kept in political subjection to the older clans. Lung Yeuk Tau in this period thus established ten new villages, until the whole of its home area was dotted with settlements, and nothing was left to be taken up by newcomers. Loi Tung established two new villages, and the only newcomers in this part of the district were a group of incoming Hakka families who settled at Man Uk Pin, which had been abandoned by the Mans.

Groups from Tan Chuk Hang founded Leng Pei, Kan Tau, and Ling Tsai in the early eighteenth century, and San Wai and San Uk Tsai a little later, leaving Tan Chuk Hang families in control of the most fertile and workable land in the centre of the main Lau Shui Heung valleys.

The Haus of Hung Leng, however, were too weak to found any new settlements of their own, nor to stop the early eighteenth century settlement of the Hakka Lee family at Lau Shui Heung in Hung Leng's immediate home territory, nor the staking out of claims to the rest of this valley by the foundation by the Lees of Ko Po and San Tong Po later in the century. Even in Hung Leng itself, the Haus were unable to stop the settlement of Hakkas, mostly Yips from Lin Ma Hang, but also Wongs and Tsangs from outside the area: by the nineteenth century, Hung Leng had become a mixed Hakka/Punti village, the only one in the area.

East of Lau Shui Heung, over the Wo Hang Au Pass, a group of Hakka families settled at Wo Hang in the later seventeenth century. Tang Sung-yi settled there a few years before 1692. In 1692, however, another family, the Lees, came to Wo Hang as well. The Lees were strong and fierce, and were determined to drive all the other families out of Wo Hang, so that they could have the whole valley for themselves. They secured the advice of a fung shui expert, and built their ancestral hall in accordance with his advice. As a result of this fung shui coup, according to both the Lees and the Tangs, the Lees were able to dominate the area, and, little by little, to drive out, or buy out, the other families.

According to the clan records of his descendants, Tang Kai-ching, the youngest son of Tang Sung-yi, feeling intimidated by the Lees' new ancestral hall, moved out of Wo Hang in 1744, and settled at the foot of the mountains in Tan Chuk Hang, where his family carved out for themselves from the forest which occupied the area the village land of Hok Tau. A generation or so later, the descendants of Tang Kai-yuen, Tang Sung-yi's eldest son, also left Wo Hang for Tan Chuk Hang, where they established themselves at Ma Mei Ha, at the entrance to the valley. The descendants of Tang Kai-cheung, Tang Sung-yi's middle son, left Wo Hang in the 1820s, and settled at Kong Ha, on reclaimed land near Sha Tau Kok Market, thus leaving the Lees effectively sole masters of the Wo Hang valley.

At about the same time as Tang Kai-tsun established himself at Hok Tau, the Wongs, another Hakka family, established themselves a short distance away from Hok Tau, at Kwai Tau Leng. Although the sites of both Hok Tau and Kwai Tau Leng were covered with forest in the middle eighteenth century, both villages have good fung shui sites, and they can thus

be confidently assumed to be older than Ma Mei Ha, which occupies a poor fung shui site. Hok Tau and Kwai Tau Leng both occupy classic fung shui sites, with fung shui woods behind them, ridges to either side, and a closed area of rice-fields in front. Hok Tau has the better fung shui site, which probably implies that it is slightly the older of the two. Ma Mei Ha, however, faces squarely down the wide open valley of the river, which runs away from the site in almost a straight line: a definitely undesirable location. The implication of this must be that no other sites were availble for settlement by the time this branch of the Tangs was looking for a new home.

The Ma Mei Ha Tangs, to minimise the negative influence of their fung shui, built a large ming-tong pond in front of the village, and planted a very thick fung shui wood in a semicircle in front of the pond, to shield the village from the bad influences likely to approach the site from down the valley. The sole access path to the village crosses this fung shui wood with a double bend, and the path is protected by earth-god shrines at both ends. From outside, the thick fung shui wood completely hid the village, and the trees looked as if they backed right up to the hill. In 1905, indeed, when the British undertook their Survey of the New Territories, Ma Mei Ha was completely overlooked, so well-hidden it was behind its screen of trees, and the Survey of Ma Mei Ha was not undertaken until 1912 in consequence.

Man Uk Pin had, by the mid-nineteenth century, become prosperous; in part because of the traffic along the main road between Shenzhen and Sha Tau Kok, which ran past the village. The fertility of the Tan Chuk Hang area had also brought prosperity to all the villages there, not only the Punti Tan Chuk Hang and its daughter villages, but also to the three

Hakka villages as well. The poorer land along the Kwan Tei River meant that the Lees of Lau Shui Heung and its daughter villages were less prosperous, and the political weakness of the Haus at Hung Leng had left them, while still comfortably off, less prosperous than before. As a result of this growing prosperity, the Lau Shui Heung villages became more of a force to be reckoned with in local politics than had been the case earlier.

In the 1860s, quarrels between the Lau Shui Heung area and the Ta Kwu Leng villages to the north came to a head. Man Uk Pin was at enmity with Ping Yeung: traffic on the Shenzhen to Sha Tau Kok road, which passed both villages, is the most likely reason, but possibly quarrels over the management of the Cheung Shan Kwu Tsz nunnery, in which both Ping Yeung and Man Uk Pin had shares, were involved as well. The nunnery was rebuilt on a new site in 1869, and negotiations over the proposed rebuilding may well have precipitated quarrels. Kwan Tei and the Tan Chuk Hang villages were also at odds with Ta Kwu Leng at the same time: free travel over the road from Kwan Tei and Tan Chuk Hang to their market at Shenzhen is the most likely reason - the villagers of this area normally crossed Ta Kwu Leng to reach Shenzhen via the ferries at Kim Hau. Lin Ma Hang, separated from Lau Shui Heung by Ta Kwu Leng, was also at odds with Ta Kwu Leng in the same period - again, free travel over the roads to the Kim Hau ferries is the most likely background.

The war between Ta Kwu Leng and the Cheungs of Wangbeiling in the 1860s is the most likely cause of these problems between Ta Kwu Leng and the Lau Shui Heung and Lin Ma Hang areas. The war was over the Kim Hau ferries, and control of the road to Shenzhen. While it was being fought - and the war must have lasted several months - the Kim Hau

THE TAN CHUK HANG VALLEY, LOOKING TOWARDS LENG PEI TSUEN AND TAN CHUK HANG   RICHARD ABRAHALL

crossings must have been effectively closed. Lin Ma Hang and Man Uk Pin must have been almost cut off from Shenzhen, and Kwan Tei and Tan Chuk Hang would have faced the much longer and less convenient route through Sheung Shui. Access to their market was vital to all villagers, and the problems of the Ta Kwu Leng war with Wangbeiling caused the Lau Shui Heung and Lin Ma Hang villages is quite enough to explain the mid-century enmity between them and the Ta Kwu Leng villages.

It is probably, therefore, to this 1860s period that the foundation of the Hung Leng Sze Yeuk ("The Alliance of Four") is to be ascribed, as a reaction to events to the north. Lin Ma Hang and Man Uk Pin formed this Yeuk alliance with Tan Chuk Hang and Kwan Tei. It was the Hakka villages of Tan Chuk Hang which were the core of the Tan Chuk Hang Yeuk: it seems likely that the Punti villages, Tan Chuk Hang itself and its daughters, only took a half share in the Tan Chuk Hang Yeuk after an initial period of hesitation. Lin Ma Hang brought Hung Leng into its Yeuk, through its lineage connection with the Yips of Hung Leng. The Haus of Hung Leng probably had a small share in the Lin Ma Hang Yeuk, as did the Yips of Hung Leng, and the Tsangs and the Wongs of that village. It is unclear what share of the Lin Ma Hang Yeuk Hung Leng held, but very probably half.

The Tan Chuk Hang Yeuk comprised two parts. Tan Chuk Hang village and its daughter villages used to meet annually to worship at the Tan Chuk Hang earth-god shrine, and these villages maintained a powerful sense of a close relationship. The villages with shares in the Tan Chuk Hang earth-god shrine probably took a half share in the Yeuk. The Hakka villages took the other half, probably divided into four equal shares, for Hok Tau, Kwai Tau Leng, Ma Mei Ha, and the Lau Shui Heung villages.

Loi Tung would have been as affected by the closure of the Kim Hau ferries as Man Uk Pin, and it is reasonable to assume that Loi Tung was as upset as Man Uk Pin at its exclusion from the market at Shenzhen by the Ta Kwu Leng and Wangbeiling war. At all events, Loi Tung took a half share in the Man Uk Pin Yeuk. Man Uk Pin and Lin Ma Hang also secured their rear by taking shares in the Sha Tau Kok Shap Yeuk, although this probably occurred a decade or so earlier than the foundation of the Sze Yeuk.

Lung Yeuk Tau would have been the least affected of the villages of the area by any closure of the Kim Hau ferries, since the normal road from Lung Yeuk Tau to Shenzhen went via Sheung Shui anyway. However, successful establishment of a new Yeuk alliance in the area traditionally dominated by Lung Yeuk Tau must have been a worry, since such Yeuk alliance areas often led to a wiping out of great clan influence in the Yeuk area. Lung Yeuk Tau accordingly decided to join the Yeuk, to attempt to steer the Yeuk away from any attempt to declare independence from Tang political dominance. Lung Yeuk Tau took, therefore, a quarter share in the Kwan Tei Yeuk.

Normally, Yeuk alliances were centred on a temple jointly owned by the allied villages, where the elders would meet to worship once a year, and to discuss the policies they would follow during the forthcoming year. Where no suitable temple existed, one would usually be founded. In the Sze Yeuk area, the alliance decided to centre itself on the ancient Hung Shing temple at Hung Leng. This must originally have been founded by the Haus of Hung Leng, but it was taken over as the temple of the Sze Yeuk, with every village of the Sze Yeuk having a share.

The Hung Leng temple was completely re-built in 1867. The donors came from every

village of the Sze Yeuk, but the managers came from Ma Mei Ha, Hok Tau, Kwai Tau Leng, plus one Hau from Hung Leng. No donor can be positively identified as coming from outside the Sze Yeuk area: none of the surnames specific to the Ta Kwu Leng area appear. The Haus, with nine donors, mostly major ones, were enthusiastic supporters of the project. The Tangs of Lung Yeuk Tau and Loi Tung provided at least thirteen donors, and very probably more. Lin Ma Hang and Man Uk Pin donated proportionally less than the other Yeuk areas.

The tablet recording the donations to the temple rebuilding includes the statement "Although the temple was established in one single village, its bright glory shines out over all the four districts." It seems very likely, given this statement, that the rebuilding of the temple marks the point when the temple ceased to be the responsibility of "one single village", and became the property of "the four districts". The temple currently has a temple keeper who has lived in the temple since the 1920s, when she was only a child. According to this lady, the document by which the villages established their Yeuk alliance used to be kept in the temple. In 1940 the temple was seriously damaged during a Japanese bombing raid on the adjacent bridge, and the document was lost. This supports the suggestion that the establishment of the Yeuk alliance was connected with the rebuilding of the temple in 1867.

Kwan Tei and Lin Ma Hang have memories of villagers who died fighting against Ta Kwu Leng, but there is no record of deaths from Man Uk Pin or Tan Chuk Hang. It seems likely that the Sze Yeuk was formally established after the Ta Kwu Leng and Wangbeiling war, with a view to the future, since a further war must have been expected for many years: Kwan Tei and Lin Ma Hang may have fought alongside

Wangbeiling individually, before the Sze Yeuk was formally established.

The essential political structure of the Sze Yeuk area was the annual feast of the Yeuk allies, which took place in front of the Hung Leng temple after the annual worship there by the elders. Each Yeuk had one table of eight places at this feast, and the number of elders from each village with places at the tables was stipulated in accordance with the shares each village had in the Yeuk. Thus Lung Yeuk Tau got two places to Kwan Tei's six, and Man Uk Pin and Loi Tung got four each. Probably Kwan Tei's six places, and Man Uk Pin's four, were distributed around the various clans in those villages according to rules agreed between the clans. The four Tan Chuk Hang Punti places were distributed among the villages of that grouping in accordance with the rules for worship at the Tan Chuk Hang earth-god: the Lung Yeuk Tau and Loi Tung places were decided on at the Tang clan gatherings of those places. At the feast the elders discussed all matters of significance affecting the area, mostly defence, but also matters such as repair of roads and bridges, and disputes between villages on water-rights or wood-cutting, or any other of the myriad problems that could sour neighbourly relations.

Lung Yeuk Tau had taken its quarter share in the Kwan Tei Yeuk probably to keep the new alliance from getting above itself. The establishment of the Yeuk certainly raised the status of the small villages, and the Tangs undoubtedly had to treat the small villages, if not as equals, then with more tact than before. Nonetheless, the essential political situation remained unchanged: Lung Yeuk Tau was just too powerful to lose its dominant position in the area. As one elder put it: "Everyone in the Yeuk was equal, and all the villages were brothers, but Lung Yeuk Tau was very fierce

and usually got its way."

Lung Yeuk Tau seems to have felt that, now the small villages had united in a yeuk, there was no need for any further patrolling of the district by the Lung Yeuk Tau militia, since the oath-sworn villages could protect themselves. Certainly, the Lung Yeuk Tau militia was not active outside Lung Yeuk Tau itself by the beginning of this century. This left the small Lau Shui Heung villages rather exposed in the explosion of cross-border banditry which afflicted the northern New Territories between 1911 and 1925, when the post-revolutionary chaos left the Shenzhen area without any effective government. Hok Tau felt sufficiently threatened by this to build itself a gun-tower. The walls of the Lung Yeuk Tau and Loi Tung villages were repaired in this same period. Tan Chuk Hang, almost surrounded by the Tan Shan River, kept its access bridge narrow and defensible. The villages of the area instituted patrols, at least in the worst times. Nonetheless, some ransom kidnappings took place, and some villages were sacked in the area at this period, despite the self-defence mechanisms in place, but the elders believe that things would have been far worse if the Yeuk alliances had not been in place.

For several hundred years, therefore, the Lau Shui Heung area had a complex history of strong and arrogant clans dominating small client villages who chafed at their lack of independence. Inter-village wars and banditry were a constant threat, fuelled by the perpetual inter-village disputes and rivalries. Oath-sworn self-defence yeuk alliances led many districts to throw off the dominance of the great clans during the nineteenth century, but the Lau Shui Heung area was too close to Lung Yeuk Tau, and had too few villages, for its Yeuk alliance to lead to full independence. Nonetheless, the council of the elders of the Yeuk alliance did

become the central political body of the area in the latter part of the nineteenth century, and the position of the smaller villages certainly improved as a result of their Yeuk alliance.

All in all, the experience of the Lau Shui Heung area typifies the vigorous and often violent politics of the traditional rural district in this region: a peaceful and bucolic existence was a traditional blessing, but one only achieved intermittently.

Dr. P.H. Hase, is a Council member of the RAS. He came to Hong Kong in 1972 and has been researching into village life and history in the area for over twenty years. He has published extensively, especially in the Journal of the Society.

HOK TAU WAI   RICHARD ABRAHALL

RICEFIELDS, HOK TAU WAI   RICHARD ABRAHALL

VEGETABLE FARMER, HOK TAU WAI   KIM APLIN

WATERING CANS AND VEGETABLE FIELDS,
HOK TAU WAI   KIM APLIN

Until a couple of decades ago, more than 90% of New Territories villagers were rice farmers, but now there are only one or two tiny plots of rice left, like this one at Hok Tau Wai, and so only a few places are left which still keep plough animals, or where it is still possible to see straw-stacks. Vegetable farmers, with their hoes and watering cans, are more common.

STRAW STACKS, HOK TAU WAI   RICHARD ABRAHALL

PLOUGH-OX, HOK TAU WAI   RICHARD ABRAHALL

HOK TAU WAI   RICHARD STOTT

HOK TAU WAI   JANET STOTT

LENG PEI TSUEN, VILLAGE SOFT DRINKS STORE   KIM APLIN

Many villages away from the main roads and New Towns still show interesting mixtures of old and new housing. Here in the Tan Chuk Hang Valley some houses are locked and barred, with the owners living abroad, but others are still inhabited. There are enough people in Leng Pei Tsuen village even to keep a soft-drinks stall in business.

HOUSES AT LENG PEI TSUEN   KIM APLIN

HOUSES AT SAN UK TSAI   KIM APLIN

HOK TAU WAI   KIM APLIN

The Headman of Hok Tau Wai built this modern house in 1969 on the site of the old brick house built by his grandfather a hundred years ago. It was one of the first modern houses in the village, but now almost all the old houses are long gone.

113

THE VILLAGE HEADMAN AND HIS GRAND-DAUGHTER,
HOK TAU WAI   RICHARD ABRAHALL

HOK TAU WAI   RICHARD ABRAHALL

HOK TAU WAI   RICHARD ABRAHALL

MA MEI HA RICHARD ABRAHALL

Most New Territories villagers are the descendants of a long line of ancestors all resident in the same place. They are truly children of the soil, and retain even today the sturdy self-reliant openness of people who know, without doubt, that they rooted where Heaven willed them to be.

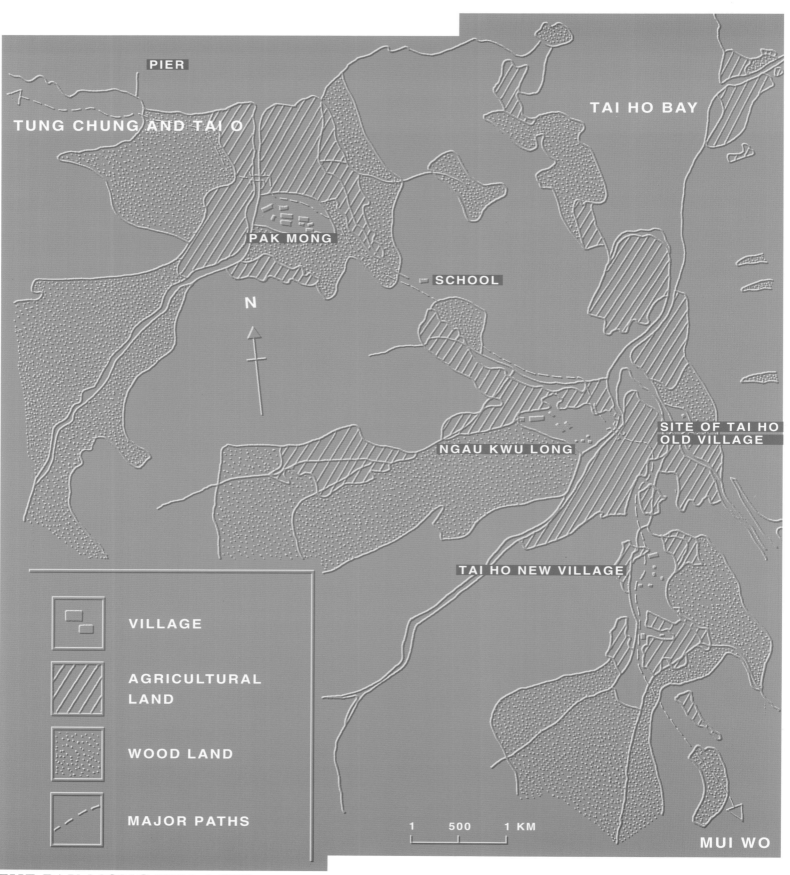

PIER

TUNG CHUNG AND TAI O

TAI HO BAY

PAK MONG

SCHOOL

N

SITE OF TAI HO
OLD VILLAGE

NGAU KWU LONG

TAI HO NEW VILLAGE

VILLAGE

AGRICULTURAL
LAND

WOOD LAND

MAJOR PATHS

1   500   1 KM

MUI WO

THE PAK MONG VILLAGES

CHAPTER SEVEN

PAK MONG, TAI HO AND NGAU KWU LONG:
THE THREE HAMLETS OF MUI WO

MA WAN   JOHN LAMBON

PAK MONG, TAI HO AND NGAU KWU LONG:
THE THREE HAMLETS OF MUI WO

JOSEPH S.P. TING*

In maps published by mainland China, Lantau Island is often referred to as Tai Ho Island, rather than as Tai Yu Shan, the more commonly used Chinese name. Tai Ho was, clearly, once a place of considerable importance.

Tai Ho is now, however, a remote and almost deserted valley, on the coast of northern Lantau, about one and a half hours walk from both Tung Chung and Mui Wo (Silvermine Bay). Tai Ho village, together with Pak Mong and Ngau Kwu Long in the same valley, are sometimes referred to as "the Three Hamlets of Mui Wo", after they were brought into the Mui Wo Rural Committee area after the War.

Four streams flowing down from the lofty mountains of central Lantau meet just below Ngau Kwu Long village ("The Cattle Pasture Valley") before entering the sea at Tai Ho Bay ("Big Oyster Bay"). Pak Mong ("White Thatcher's Grass") is a little to the west of Ngau Kwu Long, over a low pass, in an area watered by another tiny stream. The streams form small areas of flat land, sheltered from the south-west storms of summer by the main mountain ridge, and from all other directions except due north by spurs of that ridge. Dense fung shui woods protect the villages from less physical dangers from the north-west to the south, and right round to the north-east. This sheltered land once formed the paddy fields of the three villages, but all the fields are now abandoned as a result of Hong Kong's rapid development, which has drawn all the young people of the area to work in the city or overseas. The village school closed in 1986. The "kaito" service which used to run between Pak Mong and Tuen Mun ceased to operate in 1985, and with it went the

only direct contact between the villages and the outside world.

Until very recently, any hikers stepping into this seldom-visited valley were stared at with curiosity by the handful of remaining villagers, and by the herds of increasingly wild cattle descended from the animals released to freedom a decade or more ago when they ceased to be required to pull ploughs. Outsiders are likely to feel that the area is no more than a peripheral rural curiosity, but the rows of carefully and neatly laid out village houses, the strongly built watch towers, and the Maoist slogans still to be seen on the walls of some of the buildings, will suggest to the more perceptive that the area has an unusual and interesting past.

In fact, although the area has always been a remote valley on an offshore island, nonetheless, the three villages are long-settled, and have a picturesque and vivid history.

There is archaeological evidence that the indigenous Yue people settled here 4,000 years ago. Their coarse pottery *fu* - used for cooking - polished stone tools, and finely finished, polished and carved stone decorations have been found in excavations in a number of places in Lantau, including the Tai Ho valley. The settlement established by these people in the Tai Ho area seems to have survived for several thousand years.

By about 2000 years ago, the people who lived in the Tai Ho valley were using huge hard pottery jars with "seal pattern" decoration for keeping food in. They were using bronze adzes, and bronze arrow-heads for hunting. They had iron-tipped ploughs, and harvested with

crescent-shaped stone sickles. Further archaeological discoveries show that, some four hundred years later, the dead from this area were being buried richly, accompanied with deposits of grave-goods including iron scissors, green glazed jars, other bowls, and bronze coins for use in the after-life.

By the time of the Tang Dynasty, (seventh to early tenth centuries), lime was being produced by kilns from various places on Lantau, including Tai Ho, by burning coral and oyster-shells, probably for export for the white-washing of houses. Luxury products began to spread among the indigenous Lantau villages. Recently, for instance a fine export porcelain vase was uncovered: this presumably was the result of trade with the foreign ships which made Tuen Mun their normal landfall in China at this date. During this period there is growing evidence, mostly from historical records (not yet strongly supported by archaeological evidence), of settlement elsewhere in the Hong Kong area, especially around the garrison settlements at Tuen Mun, Tai Po and Kowloon, but Lantau seems still to have been among the most fully-developed and well-settled parts of the area.

In due course the imperial Government began to be interested in the Hong Kong region. The imperial salt monopoly and perhaps the imperial pearl monopoly found the waters off Lantau eminently exploitable, and, with Tuen Mun the normal port of entry to China for foreign vessels coming from the South, customs and naval patrols of the approaches were essential to imperial security.

A local Salt Commission was established

Modernisation and development are often traumatic for village communities. Here, the new Lantau Bridge towers over Ma Wan. It is, however, somehow not unexpected that, even though the bridge is founded in the soil of the island, and even though the deck of the bridge will pass right over the settlement, its residents will not be able to have access to the bridge, nor to use it to bring the full benefits of modernisation to what will remain a remote place, accessible only by ferry.

★THE AUTHOR OWES A SPECIAL DEBT OF GRATITUDE TO DR. ANTHONY SIU FOR THE GENEROUS LOAN OF GENEALOGIES OF THE VARIOUS FAMILIES RESIDING IN THE THREE HAMLETS COVERED BY THIS ARTICLE. A VOTE OF THANKS IS DUE TO THE ANTIQUITIES AND MONUMENTS OFFICE FOR ALLOWING ACCESS TO MATERIAL ON THE LATEST ARCHAEOLOGICAL DISCOVERIES. HE ALSO WISHES TO ACKNOWLEDGE DR. JAMES HAYES FOR HIS INVALUABLE ADVICE GIVEN.

PAK MONG   KIM APLIN

about 100 BC, and a Sub-Commission consisting of the Lantau coasts was in existence, by about the tenth century. A local Pearl Commission was in existence by the tenth century, and may well have had interests on Lantau, where a number of placenames (including Tai Ho) may reflect the pearling trade. The naval defences of the entry to the Pearl River consisted of concentric arcs of forts on the islands off the coast, backed up by naval patrols. The core of this system was in existence by the fourth century: by the tenth century there were almost certainly forts on Lantau as well as further out to sea.

The various administrations all had troops - in the eighth century there were already 2,000 troops headquartered at Nantou, and this figure was raised in later centuries. The various administrations also all needed labour, and the imperial might forced this out of the indigenous Yao and Tan people as unpaid labour, which was often extremely heavy.

Imperial interest in the area, therefore, led to serious problems for the long-settled inhabitants of Lantau. Even as early as 403-411 a major revolt led by Lo Hsun affected Lantau for several years. In the later twelfth century the Yao of Lantau were almost permanently in revolt because of the oppression of the salt administration: revolts are mentioned, for instance, in the historical records in 1183, 1185, 1195, and in 1197, when the Governor sent troops from Canton to "kill the people on Lantau", and again in 1200, when the troops of the Salt Commission were sent to "eradicate that nest of Yao on Lantau".

By 1200 Lantau must have been devastated, and the first settlement at Tai Ho Bay was abandoned. The whole of Lantau was granted as a reward for meritorious service to the descendants of the great Minister of State Lei Mau-ying at about this date, and the Lei family slowly found tenants to resettle the island after its earlier troubles. No trace of late Song or Yuan period (1200-1368) habitation has been found in the Tai Ho area, presumbaly reflecting the devastation of the late twelfth century revolts, and the slow re-establishment of settled life under Lei family control. However, the name of Tai Ho is found as one of the seven named villages on Lantau in a book written in the period 1573-1619 describing the area, and the bay must, therefore, have been resettled and brought back into cultivation by then. This re-established village can be called the second settlement at Tai Ho.

During the early years of the Qing dynasty (1662-1668), the Manchu court issued an order which required the coastal population to move inland, and villages within fifty *li* (Chinese miles) of the coast to be abandoned, in order to cut off any contact with the Ming Loyalist, Koxinga, in Taiwan. The order was not lifted until Koxinga was defeated six years later. But, by that time, most of the original inhabitants had either become destitute and homeless, or had been killed, or had scattered to other places. Many villages in existence before the Coastal Evacuation were unable to be re-established after the order was rescinded, including the village at Tai Ho.

An imperial edict was issued urging the original inhabitants to return and redevelop their homeland, and, when this met with an unsatisfactory response, peasants from other parts of Guangdong Province were encouraged to take up any land still lying waste. Many Hakka people, from the mountainous eastern part of Guangdong, arrived in response to this invitation. Tai Ho, Pak Mong, and Ngau Kwu Long villages were all in existence by the time the 1819 County Gazetteer was produced: all three were Hakka foundations established in the period 1723-1800. These Hakka settlers thus founded the third group of settlements at Tai Ho, which is the group of villages which still survive to the present.

The first Hakka settlers to arrive in the area, according to the villagers themselves, were the Kwok family, of Pak Mong. The Kwoks claim that they are the descendants of Guo Ziyi, a famous general of the Tang Dynasty. This clan originated in Shanghang, in Fujian Province, and the branch of the clan involved with the refoundation of Pak Mong moved later to Dabu, in Chaozhou Prefecture, Guangdong. A ninth generation ancestor of the Dabu branch settled at Pak Mong early in the eighteenth century. Five generations later, in the early nineteenth century, a descendant branched out, and established himself and his descent line at Lung Kwu Tan, near Tuen Mun. A man of the Kwok clan was a major donor to the rebuilding of the Hau Wong Temple at Tung Chung in 1911, contributing, as the commemorative inscription there shows, the substantial sum of six dollars.

The Ho clan seem to have been the next to arrive, probably in the middle of the eighteenth century. This clan originated at Ninghua in Fujian Province. Six generations later, a branch moved to Songyuan village, in Jiayingzhou County (the present Meixian County). Fourteen generations later, a branch came and settled at Tai Ho. The first settler, Ho Nam-han, was preceded by a great grand-uncle, who had settled on land a little further down the Lantau coast, at Tung Chung. It is likely that Nam-han gathered information about the prospects of this out-of-the-way but cultivable place from the descendants of this great grand-uncle before deciding to start a new life in this remote part of South China, more than 200 miles from his previous home.

The Chau clan of Tai Ho originated from Weizhou on the East River in Guangdong. Chau Hing-wah arrived at Tai Ho to take up land there late in the eighteenth century. The Lams

PAK MONG, TAI HO SAN TSUEN   KIM APLIN

PAK MONG   TONY HEDLEY

PAK MONG, RICE-DRYING GROUNDS   RICHARD STOTT

PAK MONG, NGAU KWU LONG KIM APLIN

PAK MONG, TAI HO SAN TSUEN KIM APLIN

PAK MONG KIM APLIN

For hundreds of years the small communities of North Lantau have lived their isolated and peaceful lives surrounded by the hills, woods, and streams. So remote were they that bricks were unobtainable, and the houses were built instead of small granite blocks. Now this ancient peace is shattered, as new multi-lane highways are being built across the front of the village rice-drying grounds to link the City with the new Airport, while the old agricultural instruments rot slowly away.

of Ngau Kwu Long were originally from Fujian, and later from Dongguan: the first Lam to settle in the valley probably arrived about the same time as the Chaus.

At the present, Pak Mong and Ngau Kwu Long are single lineage villages, while Tai Ho houses several clans. Ngau Kwu Long, however, has two ancestral halls, one for each of the two branches of the Lam clan settled there.

Foreign interest in this area dates from the early sixteenth century. The Portuguese occupied the Tuen Mun area from 1511 to 1523, possibly including Lantau (coastal currents require all sailing ships moving up towards Tuen Mun and the Pearl River to sail close inshore to the north coast of Lantau, making control of this coast desirable if the Portuguese were to occupy Tuen Mun). Tai Ho is the closest point on the coast of Lantau to Tuen Mun. In the early nineteenth century Pak Mong was where the ferry from Tuen Mun to Lantau landed, and this was quite probably the case in the sixteenth century as well. It is likely, therefore, that Tai Ho was affected to some degree by the Portuguese occupation: unfortunately, no archaeological evidence has yet come to light to suggest how much.

In 1794 Lieutenant Henry Parish, of the British Navy, surveyed the north Lantau coast, again because of the inshore sailing route. Parish observed that the coast was generally barren, but, at the head of one bay, where a stream of water rushed down from the hills, he noted there was some cultivation. He was probably referring to Tai Ho Bay.

In 1819 the County Gazetteer records two public ferries from Pak Mong, to Tuen Mun and Yuen Long. These were the only ferries connecting Lantau and the Mainland noted in the Gazetteer. The ferries are not mentioned in the 1688 Gazetteer, but were probably in existence long before 1819. Villagers from other places on Lantau had to travel first to Pak Mong if they wished to leave the island. Pak Mong was the gateway to Lantau. It is because the ferries came to Tai Ho Bay that the island was sometimes called Tai Ho Island. The footpaths from Pak Mong to Tung Chung and Mui Wo were, therefore, of far greater importance in those days than now. To facilitate travellers on the path from Mui Wo fine stone bridges were built over the mountain streams: one was built in 1837, as the donation tablet which still stands there details.

One might well wonder why the ferries came to Pak Mong rather than to one of the larger places on Lantau, Tai O perhaps, or Tung Chung. The most likely reason is that Pak Mong is the closest point on Lantau to Tuen Mun, thus making the ferry journey the shortest possible. Furthermore, any move of the ferry away from the Tai Ho area would have been inconvenient for Mui Wo (Pak Mong is the closest place on the north coast of Lantau to Mui Wo). There was a kaito ferry from Mui Wo to Cheung Chau, and the traffic from Cheung Chau (and from the island of Hong Kong, in the period before the British) to Tuen Mun and Yuen Long went via Mui Wo, and then across the spine of Lantau, to the ferry at Pak Mong. A further reason for the siting of the ferry was the inshore current mentioned already: any ferry leaving Pak Mong at high tide would be carried to Tuen Mun by the current, and would be less at the mercy of the winds than from other places. A counter-current at low tide would help to bring the ferry back.

After the British occupation of Hong Kong Island in 1841, the Qing authorities decided to improve the coastal defences in the vicinity, by building the Walled City at Kowloon as a headquarters garrison, and 24 smaller guard posts at various strategic places around the coast. A guard post with five soldiers was established to guard the ferry pier at Pak Mong: it was one of six along the north Lantau coast, centred on the fort at Tung Chung. The Tai Ho fort remained in operation right up to the Lease of the New Territories in 1898, eloquent testimony to the importance of the ferry routes through Pak Mong.

In 1911, a careful census gave the population of Pak Mong as 75 (40 men and 35 women), of Tai Ho as 60 (32 men and 28 women), and of Ngau Kwu Long as 85 (44 men and 41 women). The total population of the whole valley was, therefore, 220. The population remained at about this level until the abandonment of agriculture in the valley in the 1970s.

With the fall of the imperial system in China in 1911, China entered a period of unrest and lawlessness. This inevitably affected Hong Kong. In August 1911 Cheung Chau was raided by pirates, the Police Station ransacked, and the resident Policemen murdered. Other bands of pirates roamed the coasts of Lantau from time to time, crossing over from areas on the Mainland where law and order had broken down. Between 1911 and 1926 watchtowers were erected all over Lantau, to give warning of pirates. Two can still be seen in the Tai Ho valley, one on the hill overlooking Ngau Kwu Long, the other guarding the entrance to Pak Mong. According to the villagers, the village of Tai Ho, originally near the sea, had to abandon its original site, and move to a less exposed location a few hundred yards inland at about this time.

During the three years and eight months of the Japanese occupation, the villagers in the Tai Ho area suffered greatly. Since 1898 the population had grown, and a significant number of villagers had started to work as seamen, or in the city. This employment came to an end. But the fields in the village could not any longer support the whole population, and the villagers starved. Not surprisingly, the villagers were strong supporters of the anti-Japanese guerillas. Two villagers of Ngau Kwu Long were executed in Mui Wo for being guerillas, and other villagers were imprisoned, beaten, or otherwise ill-treated.

The guerillas were closely connected with Communist Party activists - in Guangdong the core of the Party after the Revolution were men who had served in the guerillas. As a result, the Tai Ho villages, like the other New Territories places with strong guerilla connections, were pro-Communist after the War. In the 1967 disturbances, therefore, the villagers supported the Maoists. Maoist slogans were painted up on many village houses, and the faded remains of them can still be seen, providing a surrealist background to those hikers from the City who stop in the villages while on a trip.

The three villages of Tai Ho were put into the Mui Wo Rural Committee after the War, providing three Village Representatives to that Committee. Before the War, the villages had managed their own affairs, and had not been part of any wider village alliance.

The villagers of the three villages share their Hakka culture and customs, and there are no differences between their way of life. They also share their remoteness and isolation: the villages are only a few hundred yards apart, but the next nearest village is more than two miles away over narrow, steep paths. Not surprisingly, the three villages are very closely intermarried. In many areas of life, the villages had to work together. The watch towers were built by the villages jointly, since any pirates who came were of equal danger to all. The village school was another joint venture, as was the ferry pier and the ferry boats, which were owned by the whole community of the three villages. Even after the population dropped to the point where the ferry was no longer viable, the few remaining villagers established a joint co-operative scheme to buy daily necessities for all of them together.

The villagers of these villages, in fact, are well-known locally for their cohesiveness and high community spirit. In 1987, of the 47 registered voters resident in the villages then, every single one cast a vote: the highest percentage of any place in Hong Kong.

The villagers of Tai Ho, Pak Mong, and Ngau Kwu Long, ever since their ancestors first settled in the valley, have maintained their living by growing rice and vegetables, with some inshore fishing, and servicing the ferries. Every family used to own a cow to plough the family fields.

The village school, at Pak Mong, had to fit its timetable to the over-riding needs of the fields. In 1968 and before, the school arranged its holidays to coincide with the harvest, with the school closed during the harvest weeks of July, and mid October - mid November, so that the children could help their parents bring in the vital grain. Rural disasters were accepted as reasons for absence from school: one girl was absent, according to the school attendance register, because she had to go into the hills to search for the family cow, which had strayed. Rural festivities, too, led to absences: on one occasion 22 of 27 students were absent, as they had all accompanied their parents to a feast at Mui Wo, on another, 32 out of 41 students were with their parents at the opera at Tung Chung. In this remote area, the whole village tended to make its rare visits to neighbouring places together, and school rules gave way before this social need.

The village continued to have a full population until the end of the 1970s. The highest number of students in the village school - 72 - was achieved in the mid 1970s. But the fields went out of cultivation in the 1970s (there was only one "farmer" father noted in the school register in 1978). Although for a few years the villagers tried to live in the village and work at Mui Wo or even off Lantau, despite the long walks this implied every day over the hills, by the 1980s the population was dropping fast, particularly of young adults with children. By 1985 the number of children in the school was down to 2, and, by the end of 1985 there were no longer any resident children of school age.

Today, the resident villagers are exclusively elderly. The younger villagers return only rarely, at village festivals, and, for most of the time the valley is quiet and empty of people. The third settlement in the Tai Ho valley would seem to be at risk of coming to an end, as did its two predecessors! However, the building of the new Airport at Chek Lap Kok, with its access road and railway, which will be built between the villages and the sea, near the site of the old ferry pier, will make a major difference. The village will be, for the first time, road accessible: some of the younger villagers will probably return to live in their native place, travelling every day to work in the Tung Chung New Town, or taking the Airport Railway to jobs in the city, which will be only a comfortable Mass Transit ride away.

Tai Ho's primeval remoteness is about to end, but, at present, the lingering remains of its long, vigorous, and occasionally even blood-thirsty history can still be sensed there.

Dr. Joseph Ting, is a Council member of the RAS and Chief Curator of the Hong Kong Museum of History.

PAK MONG   KIM APLIN

Some New Territories villages were strong supporters of the guerillas who opposed the
Japanese during the War. The guerilla groups were mostly Communist inspired, and some
of the village guerilla partisans from the New Territories became convinced Communists.
Here at Pak Mong an old guerilla has replaced his family altar with an altar to his
Communist hero.

Village houses are small, and usually windowless, the sole light and air coming through the front door. Sleeping areas are curtained off at the back, or are in cocklofts reached by ladders. There is space for only a little furniture - mostly just a few stools and a table or two, and perhaps a cupboard - although, in recent years, many houses have become full of cheaply reproduced pictures, and basic electrical equipment.

SHA LO TUNG

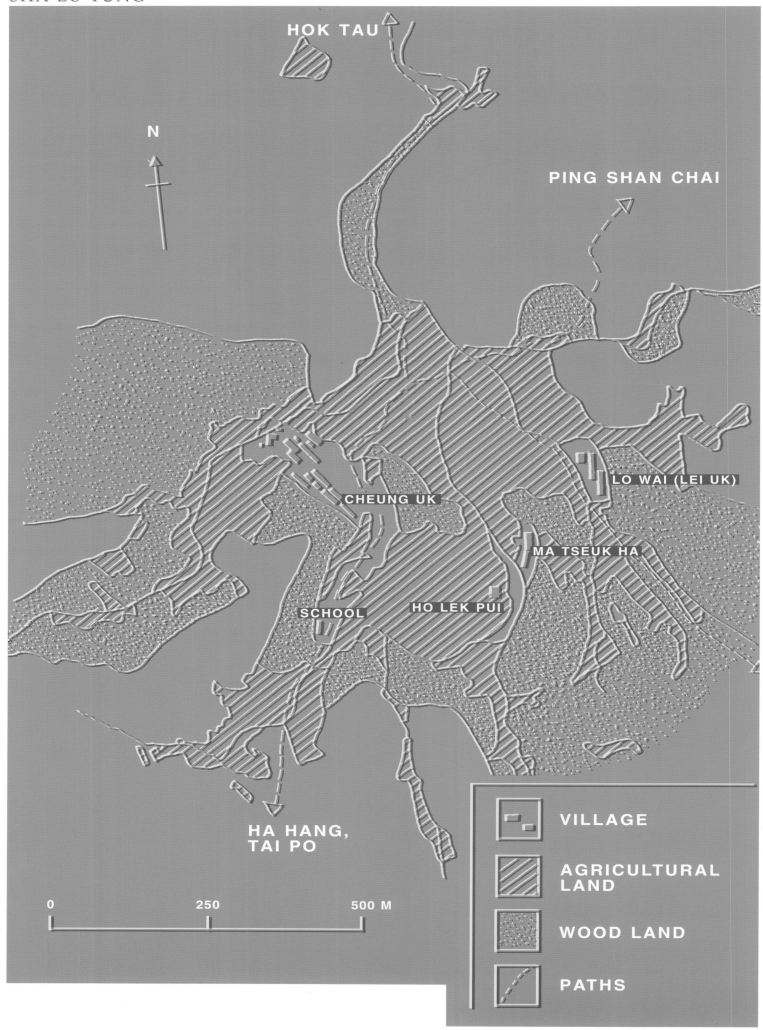

HOK TAU

N

PING SHAN CHAI

LO WAI (LEI UK)

CHEUNG UK

MA TSEUK HA

SCHOOL

HO LEK PUI

HA HANG,
TAI PO

0   250   500 M

VILLAGE

AGRICULTURAL
LAND

WOOD LAND

PATHS

CHAPTER EIGHT

SHA LO TUNG

SHA LO TUNG

RICHARD GEE

THE SETTING

The Sha Lo Tung valley and its neighbour, the Ping Shan Chai valley, form an elongated basin cradled between the western arms of the Pat Sin Ranges and the northeastern arms of Cloudy Hill, and so are protected on all four sides and completely invisible from below.

Sha Lo Tung lies to the south of the main spine of the ridges, but, nonetheless, Sha Lo Tung's lowest point is on the northern edge of the valley, where four streams meet and drain through a wooded gorge in the hills, into the Hok Tau reservoir on the northern slopes of the ridge, and so eventually into the Sham Chun River and Deep Bay. The floor of the ravine is too narrow even to accommodate a path, so the path from Sha Lo Tung to the north is carved out of its western slope. As you walk the old stone paving slabs, the stream below crashes over rocks and small waterfalls. The stream bed is a rewarding but adventurous scramble.

The Sha Lo Tung valley floor is outlined by the 180 metre contour, which traces an irregular pattern of interlinking valley floors and ridges. Old paddy fields, now abandoned but still visible, occupy every single bit of flat land.

The mountain spurs forming the valley's southern rim are 200 metres high at their lowest point, less than 20 metres above the valley floor. The ridges to the north, however, are much higher, reaching 450 metres in places. The 1929 (revised 1938) 1:20,000 map shows four paths out. Three linked Sha Lo Tung with the Tai Po area to the south. One, south of Cheung Uk, led directly south down the hill to Fung Yuen. 200 metres to the east, the second, roughly parallel to the first, led to Ha Hang on the coast, and was later replaced by the modern road. The third path, south of Lei Uk, led down a valley to Shuen Wan. The fourth path led north, beside the stream, to Hok Tau, and so on to Sham Chun and Sha Tau Kok.

HISTORY

Sha Lo Tung was settled by two Hakka migrant clans - the Cheungs and the Leis - who came into this area from further north in the late 1600s and early 1700s, following the Coastal Evacuation of 1662-1669. Their movement over the generations (first into Guangdong province, then into the Pearl River delta, on into the Hong Kong area, and finally into Sha Lo Tung) is a pattern repeated all over Hong Kong. The earlier Punti people probably had no interest in this remote upland valley.

The Cheung clan were the first to arrive here, probably about 300 years ago. Their genealogy contains only the briefest details of names, and no dates, so a little guesswork is required to reconstruct past events. It is said to have been compiled in 1953, based on earlier versions dating from 1700, the 39th year of the Qing Emperor Kangxi's reign.

It records 19 generations in the Sha Lo Tung branch of the clan, from 1953 back to the founding ancestor who was buried in Chaozhou, in northeastern Guangdong province. Assuming 25-30 years between generations, that places the founding ancestor in the early mid-15th century, in the first half of the Ming dynasty. Five generations lived there, before the sixth generation (probably in the latter part of the Ming dynasty) moved to Dongguan, on the Pearl River estuary between Hong Kong and Canton. The genealogy records that an eighth generation wife was the first family member to be buried in Sha Lo Tung, so we can guess that one branch of the clan moved to Sha Lo Tung in the eighth generation, sometime in the late seventeenth century, probably very shortly after the Coastal Evacuation.

The Cheungs first settled at Lo Wai ("the Old Village"), at the foot of a spur of the Pat Sin Range on the eastern side of the valley. This is a constricted site, having room for only two or three rows of houses, raised just a few feet above the fields.

The Lei clan settled in Sha Lo Tung rather later, in the early 1700s. Their genealogy is much more precise than that of the Cheungs, and gives detailed information and dates. The Leis trace their origin back to Dingzhou, in Fujian province, from where they migrated south to Guangdong to escape the disturbances that came with the fall of the Yuan dynasty in the mid-13th century. Lei Tsz-ching (1656-1728), of the 15th generation, moved to the Tai Po area in 1689 and settled in Wai Ha, in Shuen Wan, a mile and a half over the ridge southeast of Sha Lo Tung. Here he brought up his four sons.

Lei Tsz-ching's oldest son, Lei Wai-yan (1684-1770), made a living collecting shells from the rivers up in the hills and, while visiting Sha Lo Tung, he took a fancy to one of the Cheung family girls (presumably from their tenth generation). They got married, and his parents-in-law urged Lei Wai-yan to move up to Lo Wai and live near them. This was an unusual idea, but perhaps it was more convenient for his work and there was a good deal of potentially good arable land still available for development there. Lei Wai-yan thus became the first Lei clan member to settle in Sha Lo Tung where he had three sons. Lei Wei-yan later brought the body

Christian missionaries, both Catholic and Protestant, have made converts in the villages for well over a hundred years.

SHA LO TUNG, CHEUNG UK   RICHARD STOTT

SHA LO TUNG, LEI UK RICHARD STOTT

Even though they have been abandoned for a decade, or even a generation, the village rice fields are still recognisable, although scrub is beginning to invade, and drainage systems to clog and flood. Here the fung shui wood, village, and fields remain to be seen, but further decay may soon destroy beyond recognition this three hundred year old scene.

of his great-grandfather from the family's previous home, and reburied him at Sha Lo Tung, thereby demonstrating this family's commitment to its new home. The path to Shuen Wan, which passed Wai Ha where the descendants of Lei Wai-yan's brothers continued to live, used to go along the valley south of Lo Wai, and must have been much used by members of the two branches of the Lei clans.

After some time, the Cheung family came to the conclusion that the fung shui of Lo Wai was not good for them. They decided to move, and chose a larger site on the western side of the valley. Cheung Uk ("the Cheung Clan village"), 500 metres west of Lo Wai, was therefore the second settlement in the valley. Most of it is built on a slightly raised area of land at the foot of a spur of Cloudy Hill, where the Cheungs thought the fung shui would be better. It faces northeast, protected behind and on both sides by ridges, and with the gap in the hills to the north well disguised by trees. After the move of the Cheungs to Cheung Uk, Lo Wai and its daughter settlements eventually became known as Lei Uk.

Only two or three houses in Lo Wai are visible from Cheung Uk; the rest are hidden behind the low rise in the centre of the valley. The two families have different opinions about the fung shui of Cheung Uk; according to the Leis it is not good, and causes young men to die. A division of the valley between the two clans may well have been involved in the move of the Cheungs. The valley remained, however, a unit: for instance, there was always one school, serving the whole valley. When this was rebuilt in the 1950s, it was built at the junction of the paths, equally convenient to both clans.

According to the Leis, the descendants of Wai-yan's second son established Ma Tseuk Ha in the early nineteenth century. Ma Tseuk Ha is 200 metres southwest of Lo Wai, at the foot of another spur and right next to a stream. Here

there was room for only one row of houses, with a common courtyard in front. Later still (possibly in the early twentieth century), the third son's descendants established Ho Lek Pui, opposite Ma Tseuk Ha on the western side of the stream. The descendants of Lei Wai-yan's eldest son remained at Lo Wai.

When Lei Wai-yan first settled at Lo Wai, the total population of Sha Lo Tung was very small - probably no more than a couple of dozen people - and much potentially arable land remained uncleared and covered in forest. As the population slowly grew, during the eighteenth and nineteenth centuries, so more and more of the arable land was brought under cultivation. By the late nineteenth century, all arable land was under cultivation, and the population had begun to exceed the subsistence capacity of the valley.

The Sha Lo Tung villagers marketed at Tai Po. This market was owned by the wealthy and ancient Tang clan of Tai Po Tau. The Tangs had founded, or, more probably, refounded, the market in 1672, after the Coastal Evacuation. They demanded toll from all non-Tang users of the market, and insisted on Tang purchasers getting certain advantages (especially the right of priority of purchase) over others. The villagers of the area had long sought to end this Tang monopoly, but the Tangs were able to crush all attempts to found a rival market until 1893-96 when a coalition of the non-Tang villagers successfully established a new market (the present day Tai Po Market), and built a bridge over the river, across the line of the ferry previously owned by the Tangs. The village coalition was a federation of seven oath-sworn inter-village mutual defence associations, and was known as the Tsat Yeuk ("Alliance of Seven") in consequence.

The Sha Lo Tung villagers had a share in one of the Seven Yeuk, and had an interest in the new market as a result; the growing need to secure income from marketing fuel and other

mountain products, to offset their lack of rice, doubtless spurred the Sha Lo Tung villagers to join the anti-Tang coalition.

In 1898, the British took over the whole area, calling it the "New Territory". In 1899 soldiers came to establish British authority. The Tangs and the Tsat Yeuk set aside their differences to organise resistance, which culminated in April 1899 with the Battle of Tai Po. Nearly all the resistance leaders were Punti people, from clans settled nearby for almost a thousand years, especially the Tangs. However, there were two leaders from the Leis of Sha Lo Tung. So despite its limited arable land and poor access, Sha Lo Tung was well assimilated into local affairs.

No harm came to anyone from Sha Lo Tung because of its involvement in the Battle of Tai Po. Between 1900 and 1950 the village maintained its subsistence rice cultivation and market town trading lifestyle. The new British connection, however, made it easier for villagers to find jobs abroad, or in the city, or as seamen, and a substantial percentage of the adult male Sha Lo Tung villagers took advantage of this.

By 1911, as shown in the Census for that year, only 127 of the 307 persons then resident in Sha Lo Tung were male (41%) - probably nearly half the adult males were by that date usually resident outside the valley.

On December 8th, 1941, the Japanese invaded Hong Kong. In the initial hours of the invasion, the Japanese 229th Infantry Regiment passed through Sha Lo Tung on its way to Kowloon, climbing up the Hok Tau path and then on to Tai Po by the old path through Fung Yuen. The damage caused by the passage of the Japanese was a foretaste of the difficulties Sha Lo Tung, like so many other mountainside villages in the New Territories, was to experience during the years of the Japanese occupation. For two generations, the valley had become in part dependent on remittances from villagers overseas, and these could not be received any more. Hunger and privation were the outcome. Sha Lo Tung, however, had more riceland than most mountainside villages, so starvation and death from famine did not become common here.

After the War, the old pattern re-established itself - rice subsistence agriculture, augmented by remittances from villagers living in the city or overseas. In 1958, according to the Hong Kong Gazetteer, there were 74 resident families, with 442 persons, and in 1960, according to the Hong Kong Gazetteer of Place Names, there were 445 residents, 260 in Cheung Uk, and 185 in the Lei Uk villages.

During the late 1960s and 1970s, however, rice farming in places like Sha Lo Tung became unviable. More and more of the villagers left. By the mid 1970s the village was home to only a few dozen elderly residents, dependent on remittances. Agriculture, with the exception of a few fields of sugar-cane, had come to an end, and with it Sha Lo Tung's three hundred years as a viable community.

A TOUR OF THE VILLAGES

The buildings of Sha Lo Tung display many typical elements of Chinese architecture, but all the buildings are being attacked by ants and morning glory. Winter provides the easiest access to the ruins. Significant elements to look out for include layout, walls, doors, windows, roofs, external decorations, and interiors.

CHEUNG UK

Cheung Uk is a fine example of a traditional New Territories unwalled village with parallel rows of houses. The present length from northwest to southeast is 170 metres, but ruins at both ends show that there used to be three dozen more houses, making a total length of 270 metres. The widest part is 80 metres from front to back, with seven distinct rows separated by narrow lanes. The southeastern end of the village and the front line of houses are at the same level as the surrounding fields, but the rest of the village is raised slightly on a gentle slope.

From a distance what stands out are the roofs of Cheung Uk. These show regularity of direction and pitch; the many minor variations add to rather than detract from the overall cohesiveness. There are only two modern buildings. The flat-roofed one in the back row stands out clearly. The one in the front row, with a roof at the same angle as all the others, blends in more even though it has two storeys; however, it lacks the traditional curve and point on the roof-ends.

Some buildings have a different roof pattern because they have a small interior courtyard behind the front door, open to the sky, but not visible from outside when the door is closed. Light coming in through the open courtyard is enough to light the rooms inside and make external windows unnecessary - good for security, and possibly giving better air circulation. Cheung Uk has several good examples of this layout at the northwestern ends of the front and second rows.

Some of the houses in Cheung Uk are well-built, and reflect the wealth some of the villagers gained by working outside the village. The owners displayed this wealth by building walls with good quality bricks that do not need plastering. They have panels at the tops of the walls which were originally brightly painted, or carried carved stucco decorations. The village must have looked very colourful when they were all freshly painted, since many of the old houses have such panels. The roof overhangs a little to protect the decorations from the rain. The open yards in front of the houses are for drying rice, working, or just sitting out in the sun. Most of the village houses have such an open yard, no matter how small.

Entering one of these wealthier houses, you find yourself in the interior courtyard. The recess in the floor collects rainwater, which drains out through an underfloor drain. To your right is the kitchen, to your left a store-room. Ahead is the main living room. When the houses were still lived in, the family altar would usually have been opposite you on the back wall. To your right and left are other living and working rooms, with cocklofts above, used for sleeping or storage.

Throughout Sha Lo Tung, the older buildings have small windows, so high that it is impossible to see inside. They give only a little light, but they do give maximum security. Windows high in the back wall are often just tiny holes without glass. A few houses, both in Cheung Uk and in Lei Uk, have small square ceramic frame windows in front.

South of the village, near the end of the access road from Tai Po, is the government school, built in the 1950s when there were enough children in Sha Lo Tung to warrant two schoolrooms. The access road is private; it has never been adopted by the government because it does not meet public standards.

THE CHEUNG CLAN
ANCESTRAL HALL

The main Cheung clan ancestral hall is in the southeasternmost block of Cheung Uk village. This block is purpose-built; it has a distinctive roof pattern, but the part at the back is only one storey high, unlike the courtyard houses, where the back block is usually two storeyed. The construction of the hall is better than any other building in the village. Solid stone door posts and much fine brickwork convey its importance. In 1983, it was restored after being damaged in a typhoon.

The doors of the ancestral hall are mostly locked, but when they are open, you can see the interior courtyard stretching back to the clan altar on the far wall. In the usual Hakka style, it has just one name tablet on the altar which

SHA LO TUNG, CHEUNG UK   RICHARD STOTT

SHA LO TUNG, CHEUNG UK   RICHARD STOTT

SHA LO TUNG, CHEUNG UK   RICHARD ABRAHALL

Many village houses had a tiny walled-in courtyard in front of the main entrance, where the household cooking took place, and where the farm implements were stored. Other houses roofed this area over. Many families occupied two, or even three, house units, opening doorways between the front courtyards of the houses. These neat houses, with their fine brick frontages and stout tile roofs, backed by the spreading branches of the fung shui trees, remain visually extremely satisfying.

SHA LO TUNG, CHEUNG UK   RICHARD ABRAHALL

SHA LO TUNG, CHEUNG UK   RICHARD ABRAHALL

Nowadays, only a few old women still live at Sha Lo Tung. They, like the women of previous generations, still cut wood to fuel their cooking fires, and they still dry vegetables during the Summer for the Winter. They still wear the Hakka head-dresses so typical of the New Territories.

honours the whole clan. To the right, a big hanging lantern swings in the breeze. On the left-hand wall, a plaque records the names of those who financed the reconstruction. Behind the door is an old chicken-coop, used in clan marriage rituals.

MA TSEUK HA

The path to Lei Uk starts opposite the school, and with the aid of boards in difficult places, follows the stream around the southern edge of the valley. Ma Tseuk Ha is the first group of houses - two blocks, with a long communal courtyard in front, and two fishponds (now overgrown and invisible) in front of the courtyard.

The structure of these houses is much simpler than those of Cheung Uk. None of them have interior courtyards. In fact, they have been squeezed onto this narrow strip of land only by cutting away the hillside behind. Between the north and south blocks is a little open space, bricked off at the front and accessible only from the houses on each side.

These houses lie abandoned as the villagers left them, often with the dishes of the last meal still on the tables.

HO LEK PUI

The isolated building on the other side of the stream is all that is left of Ho Lek Pui, the newest part of Lei Uk. It is accessible by walking across the weir south of the houses and pushing through the trees and grass. The left-hand half contains a good number of traditional farming tools, while the right-hand half has a layout not seen in any of Sha Lo Tung's other buildings. Half-screened upper rooms at both back and front are joined by a balustraded landing along one wall. On the opposite wall to the landing, flaking plaster has exposed the bricks. They are much bigger than any others

in Sha Lo Tung, and are a reminder that this house was built at a different time.

LO WAI

Between Ma Tseuk Ha and Lo Wai, the path passes Sha Lo Tung's biggest grave, 9 metres wide and 12 metres from front to back. There are graves, burial urns, pots and huts scattered on the hillsides around Sha Lo Tung valley in hundreds of locations.

The final approach to Lo Wai is through a perennially wet paddy and damp courtyard. Sha Lo Tung's oldest houses have almost vanished under morning glory and long grasses. The two more modern units at the front are starting to go the same way.

According to the Leis, Lo Wai grew from left to right. The southern, newer, block was built as a series of interior courtyard houses, one of which was the Lei clan ancestral hall, identifiable by the offerings on the table and the writing above the door. Visitors have stolen the ancestral tablet, and the offerings are infrequently renewed. I am told that the ancestral trust, although it has enough money for upkeep, is in weak hands, and that the older generation no longer seem to care.

Two units to the left of the ancestral hall of the Lei clan is another ancestral hall, of the Cheung clan. Lo Wai was the Cheungs' original home and this hall was maintained for a long time after they moved across the valley, even though a new hall was built at Cheung Uk.

THE NATURAL ENVIRONMENT

Sha Lo Tung has a unique natural environment. Why? In part this is due to the isolation of the valley, particularly after the desertion of the villages. However, the valley has other special natural features as well. A Position Paper prepared by environmental groups in August 1994 noted that "the valley

is well wooded and watered, crossed by at least 4 streams and numerous tributaries which are slow moving and some of which merge into extensive areas of wetland or old paddy and grassland. This unusual variety of habitat, together with the unusual and important upland wet areas supports exceptionally high biological diversity." Giving specific details of the biodiversity, the Paper states that "Sha Lo Tung supports over half of the butterfly and amphibian species in Hong Kong. Almost 50 percent of the larger mammals and dragonflies of Hong Kong occur at Sha Lo Tung. A number of protected species are also recorded at Sha Lo Tung. In addition, species new to science and Hong Kong have also been discovered at Sha Lo Tung."

The Paper's count of species noted in Sha Lo Tung includes 171 species of medicinal plants, and 583 species of vascular plants. It includes barking deer, civets, wild boar, leopard cats, the Javan mongoose, ferret badger, pangolin, and porcupine. It includes 3 species of bats, 113 species of birds, 8 species of lizards, 10 species of snakes, and 11 species of amphibians. It also includes 39 species of dragonflies (including two new to science), and 112 species of butterflies. A further 128 species of butterfly have been recorded in the Fung Yuen valley, south of Sha Lo Tung; the wooded hillside on the northern end of Fung Yuen valley has been designated a Site of Special Scientific Interest to protect their habitat.

MODERN SHA LO TUNG, AND THE GOLF COURSE PROJECT

In 1979 a developer decided that Sha Lo Tung would be a good site for an 18-hole golf-course and luxury residential area development. The agricultural land would form the core of the golf-course, although the developers assumed that government would release a further 77 acres (31 hectares) of government land from the adjacent Country Park to make the golf-course viable. 350 luxury houses and apartments, and 160 new houses for the villagers were to be built. The narrow access road would be rebuilt and widened. A small part of Cheung Uk was to be restored as a "heritage centre". The villagers were urged by the developer to sell their land: the terms were $12 per square foot for the agricultural land, a new house for each villager, preservation of the Cheung clan ancestral hall, and a $3 million welfare donation to each of the two clans. Most of the villagers accepted these terms, took the money for the agricutlural land, and went to live in Tai Po for what they assumed would be a short wait for the new houses.

However, the developer froze the scheme during the 1980s, because of local economic problems, and it was only at the very end of the 1980s that formal planning consent was sought from the government.

In 1990 the government agreed to release the necessary Crown and Country Park land. But in 1991, environmental groups and the media learned about the plan; what they saw was the government giving public recreational land to private commercial interests, in apparent dereliction of its duty under the Country Parks Ordinance. Furious, they organised resistance. As a result, the government ordered the developers to revise their plans, and to produce an Environmental Impact Assessment Report.

The developers have revised the plan, which now involves no Country Park land, although they still need Crown land. The proposal is now for a 9 hole, not 18-hole, golf-course. The ridge behind Cheung Uk is now proposed to be set aside as a 7.8 hectare "wildlife conservation area with associated nature trails". The 259-page EIA report issued in June 1993, said that damage would be minimal. Environmental groups remain vigorously opposed, however, and the government has not yet made a decision on the revised proposals.

The most recent plans (for a 9-hole golf course) envisage a club house at the southern end of the central wooded rise in the middle of the valley, in front of Cheung Uk. The fairways would occupy the old paddy fields to the west of the rise, and the valleys behind Cheung Uk and north of Lei Uk. The new village houses would be in the flat valley south of the school, with separate areas for the Cheungs and the Leis. On the eastern valley fringe, where Lei Uk presently stands, would be the luxury houses and apartments.

Some of the Cheung Uk's houses would be restored. Unfortunately, there is little sensitivity to the details as currently proposed. The restoration would retain little sense of the existing village and its layout. The 1993 plan indicates a single line of restored buildings, running from the ancestral hall in the southeast. It would provide facilities for a conservation education centre, a heritage centre, and a shop and toilets. To the north would be a bird of prey study centre; to the south, "working paddy fields". The ancestral hall would be converted into "a place of worship available for the general public". Finally, they would create "a paved courtyard with a traditional banyan tree at its centre".

The grounds for opposition by environmentalists have shifted. Initially they were based on the government's perceived neglect of its duty, and the impact that the project would have on the surrounding area - mainly visual but also ecological, such as the risk of polluting Hok Tau Reservoir. But as both sides have done more studies, Sha Lo Tung has emerged as a unique and irreplaceable environmental niche.

The World Wide Fund for Nature Hong Kong propose that Sha Lo Tung should be designated a Site of Special Scientific Interest. Friends of the Earth propose it should be designated a Protected Wetland Area under Articles 7 and 8 of the Convention on Biological Diversity (an international legal framework like that which it has been agreed should protect Mai Po Marshes).

The government has not responded to either of these ideas. At present the government has the plan under discussion in a study group with representatives from three government departments.

The villagers, however, are now extremely upset. They feel they are being treated very badly. The developers have not built their new village as they promised in 1979. Worse, if the conservationists win their case to designate Sha Lo Tung as a Site of Special Scientific Interest, the villagers might even lose the right to build or rebuild their own houses. In frustration, the Lei family gave the developer an ultimatum in 1994 - build the new houses, or they will build their own. The Cheungs support the Leis. An action committee of the villagers is building support for their position. A petition has been drawn up, which has so far collected 200 signatures. This petition demands that either the developer builds them their new houses as promised in 1979, or they are allowed to build their own. The villagers are anxious to get it all resolved before 1997.

What the future holds for this uniquely beautiful valley remains unclear. But in its ruined, but untouched, condition it still offers today a window into its agricultural past. With age, this has mellowed to become a natural environmental sanctuary, of the greatest value. All this will change, but to what, or how far, no-one yet knows.

Richard Gee is a member of the RAS and Managing Director of Reading Strategies Limited, which teaches people to learn, think and read more effectively. He is author of *Rambles in Hong Kong*.

SHA LO TUNG, LEI UK   KIM APLIN

SHA LO TUNG, CHEUNG UK   RICHARD ABRAHALL

Termites, fire, rain, and typhoon can quickly turn even the best-built
village houses into ruins within a few decades, if they are uninhabited and
left without maintainence. It is usually the roofs which break first,
as the pinewood beams and rafters need constant attention against termites
and damp.

Often, villagers did not expect to leave their houses for good. They left the doors carefully locked and barred, and all their possessions in their places. But they never came back, and the irreversible decay slowly overtakes everything; doors and stove-god shrines, agricultural implements, the pots on the family stove, and most evocative of all, the family clock, lying broken on the floor where it fell when the nail on which it hung rusted through. "Time stands for ever still".

SHA LO TUNG, CHEUNG UK   RICHARD ABRAHALL

SHA LO TUNG, CHEUNG UK   RICHARD ABRAHALL

SHA LO TUNG TONY HEDLEY

SHA LO TUNG RICHARD ABRAHALL

CHEUNG UK, RICHARD ABRAHALL

SHA LO TUNG, CHEUNG UK RICHARD ABRAHALL

STOVE-GOD, SHA LO TUNG, CHEUNG UK RICHARD ABRAHALL

SHA LO TUNG, CHEUNG UK RICHARD ABRAHALL

SHA LO TUNG, LEI UK KIM APLIN

A STOVE, SHA LO TUNG, CHEUNG UK RICHARD ABRAHALL

SHA LO TUNG TONY HEDLEY

147

ANCESTRAL PORTRAITS, SHA LO TUNG, CHEUNG UK   RICHARD ABRAHALL

THE PLOUGH STILL HANGS WAITING TO BE USED, EVEN THOUGH THE ROOF HAS FALLEN IN, SHA LO TUNG, CHEUNG UK   RICHARD ABRAHALL

SHA LO TUNG, CHEUNG UK   RICHARD ABRAHALL

SHA LO TUNG, CHEUNG UK   RICHARD ABRAHALL

SHA LO TUNG, CHEUNG UK   RICHARD ABRAHALL

INSIDE AN ABANDONED HOUSE, SHA LO TUNG   KIM APLIN

153

SHA LO TUNG KIM APLIN

SHA LO TUNG KIM APLIN

SHA LO TUNG KIM APLIN

SHA LO TUNG KIM APLIN

SHA LO TUNG KIM APLIN

SHA LO TUNG KIM APLIN

SHA LO TUNG, CHEUNG UK RICHARD STOTT

SHA LO TUNG, CHEUNG UK KIM APLIN

SHA LO TUNG KIM APLIN

The old houses at Sha Lo Tung contain many remains of traditional village life: cooking vessels, clothes, a decorated chicken coop used to carry wedding gifts of poultry, a chair made by a village craftsman, and a neatly woven rattan basket. An old almanac finds itself next to a broken clock. Time, seasons, and the years themselves have all passed by since these houses were full of vibrant life.

SHA LO TUNG   KIM APLIN

SHAN HA WAI
[TSANG TAI UK]

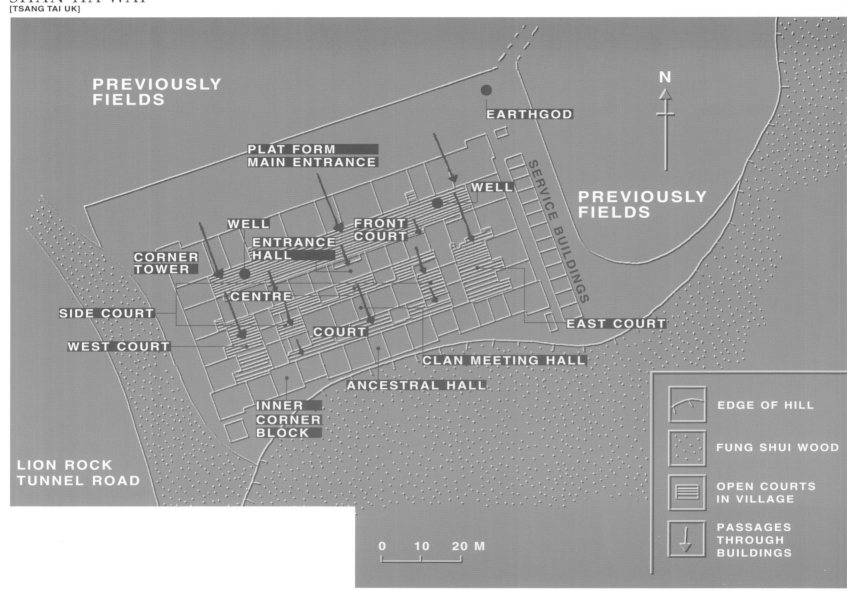

PREVIOUSLY
FIELDS

EARTHGOD

N

PLAT FORM
MAIN ENTRANCE

WELL

PREVIOUSLY
FIELDS

SERVICE BUILDINGS

WELL

FRONT
COURT

ENTRANCE
HALL

CORNER
TOWER

CENTRE

EAST COURT

SIDE COURT

WEST COURT

COURT

CLAN MEETING HALL

ANCESTRAL HALL

INNER
CORNER
BLOCK

LION ROCK
TUNNEL ROAD

0   10   20 M

EDGE OF HILL

FUNG SHUI WOOD

OPEN COURTS
IN VILLAGE

PASSAGES
THROUGH
BUILDINGS

CHAPTER NINE

TSANG TAI UK

TSANG TAI UK   RICHARD ABRAHALL

TSANG TAI UK

ROSEMARY LEE

The tradition of building walled towns and planned villages is very ancient in China. As long ago as the Warring States Period, Chou Li Kao Kung Chi outlined the planning principles, including the customs and rituals, that should be observed when building such defended places. Whilst the architecture of palaces, and imperial temples and tombs, reflecting the imperial way of life, has been more studied and is better known, walled villages reflecting the vernacular culture of the ordinary people can still be seen here and there.

This vernacular walled village tradition has existed for many centuries in the New Territories, where there are several fine examples. Perhaps the most interesting of these, Tsang Tai Uk or, more properly, Shan Ha Wai, is at Sha Tin. Completed in the 1870s, and occupying 60,000 square feet, with its massively high and fortified walls, gun slits and watch towers at each of the four corners of its uncompromisingly four square design, it is an outstanding and formidable example, even though, as the construction of an immigrant outsider, its layout differs from most other Hong Kong walled villages, which follow more indigenous traditions.

The Tsang Clan has an ancient genealogy which claims an unbroken descent from the Shang Dynasty when the Emperor Shao Kang granted his son, Qu Lie, the State of Tsang. The Spring and Autumn Annals recount that a descendant Tseng Mau was defeated in battle but escaped, and changed his family name to Tsang. Whether any of the Tsangs resident in the New Territories today in fact have a blood connection with Tsang Mau is a moot point, but most of the Tsang clans in the New Territories,

both Punti and Hakka, claim descent from him, including both the Hakka founder of Tsang Tai Uk, Tsang Koon-man, and the Punti Tsangs of Kak Tin from whom he bought the land on which it stands. According to the other Sha Tin villagers, it was this claimed common descent from Tsang Mau which eventually induced the Kak Tin Tsangs to sell the land to Tsang Koon-man, where other local clans had refused to sell him any.

Tsang Koon-man (also known as Tsang Sam-li), who built and designed Tsang Tai Uk as a residence for a self-contained single clan extended family unit, was a Hakka from the present day Changle District in north-east Guangdong Province. Many Hakka from this area had come to the Hong Kong area in the late eighteenth and early nineteenth centuries to work quarries, especially in the Kwun Tong and Quarry Bay areas. The granite they quarried was carried to Guangzhou for sale in many boats operating from Kowloon City and Shau Kei Wan. Some relatives of Tsang Koon-man had set up in the Kowloon City area before 1824 in this trade. Tsang Koon-wah was born in 1808 in impoverished circumstances. As he grew up he heard of the opportunities in the Kowloon City area, and he and his brother came to seek a livelihood there in 1824, when Tsang Koon-man was 16. Initially they worked as cooks in a quarry at Cha Kwo Ling but Tsang Koon-man soon became foreman.

Shortly after, but before the British takeover of Hong Kong Island, Tsang Koon-man moved to Shau Kei Wan where he set up a quarry, the Sam-li Quarry. He also founded a shop. Both these businesses continued to exist as Tsang family concerns for many decades. Tsang Koon-

man also sold fresh water to junks, and the family also ran a cargo boat.

Tsang Koon-man was, therefore, in an excellent position to profit from the huge demand for building stone created by the establishment of Hong Kong, and he quickly became prosperous by meeting Hong Kong's insatiable demands for building materials.

Tsang Koon-man's descendants tell other, more romantic, versions of the sources of Tsang Koon-man's wealth as well as this tale of hard work in a quarry which eventually proved to be well located. They tell of some seamen who left several jars filled with salt fish with Tsang Koon-man for safe-keeping. The seamen did not return, so eventually Tsang took out some of the fish from the jars and found a cache of silver bars hidden beneath. He assumed the seamen were pirates who had come to a bad end. Tsang Koon-man thereupon used this windfall to expand his business, and became wealthy as a result.

Tsang Koon-man's prosperity, whatever its source, can be seen from his donations to the rebuilding of the Tin Hau Temple in Shau Kei Wan in 1872, when he was the largest single donor, and to the further repairs to the same temple in 1876, when he was one of the managers of the project. (In 1920 Tsang Koon-man's sons were also prominent in the repairs to this temple of that year.) Above all, however, his prosperity can be seen from the foundation of Tsang Tai Uk.

Tsang Koon-man decided in 1848 to find land to buy on which he could establish a village for his descendants. Three questions need to be asked: why did this quarry-owner want to found a village, why did he choose Sha

Tsang Tai Uk was built by a wealthy Hakka quarryman of Shau Kei Wan, in the style of his home district far away in the north-east of Guangdong. Strong and imposing, with its elegant corner towers, gates, and gun-ports, it breathes a very antique air, although it was only built 125 years ago.

TSANG TAI UK, FRONT FACE   RICHARD STOTT

TSANG TAI UK, FRONT FACE   RICHARD ABRAHALL

TSANG TAI UK, FRONT FACE   RICHARD STOTT

Tsang Tai Uk is built of good granite and fine brick, and stands austere and almost without decoration, except for the engraved couplets around the entrance gates. Above the gates are cannon-ports, and the whole length of the roofline is pierced with gun-ports, although the village never had enough guns to arm each one. The central gate has an inscription over it "A residence for endless generations", which encapsulates the founder's hopes and wishes.

Tin and why did he build it with defensible walls and gates?

In traditional China, life as a merchant, such as Tsang Koon-man, was not only viewed as less dignified than life as a farmer, but less secure as well. Sooner or later there might be a depression and the bankrupt merchant would have to watch his children starve. But the owner of farm land would never starve so long as the ground survived out of which the rice grew. Tsang Koon-man was, in part, investing his wealth in land which would keep his descendants no matter how things turned out. At the same time, only a very successful and prosperous merchant could afford to buy riceland sufficient to keep a whole village, and to build residences enough for many generations of his descendants. The foundation of Tsang Tai Uk was, therefore, also a public affirmation of Tsang Koon-man's success and wealth.

At the same time, Tsang Koon-man was, like many merchants in traditional China, eager to improve his social status. He was eventually to buy an imperial degree, and his ownership of fields and rural houses must have made his advancement in the highly conservative world of late imperial China easier, as he could be seen as a farmer and scholar rather than as an artisan and merchant. So it is easy to understand why Tsang Koon-man decided to buy riceland and found a village.

Today Sha Tin is a busy New Town of some three quarters of a million people, but in the nineteenth century the population for the whole of the New Territories was only about 100,000, and Sha Tin was a purely rural valley. At the same time, the Sha Tin area has a long history and it is known, for instance, that there were walled Punti villages at Tai Wai and Tin Sam from the Ming Dynasty. After the Coastal Evacuation many Hakkas had established villages in the area: by 1848 probably two-thirds of the population of Sha Tin was Hakka.

Sha Tin in the nineteenth century was a rich agricultural area. Not until the end of the Pacific War in 1945 did Shatin's agricultural prosperity decline when it became more economical to import rice from South-east Asia. Tsang Koon-man invested in the land at Tsang Tai Uk because it was the best available agricultural land - or at least the best available land with a substantial Hakka resident population - easily accessible from the city. Here he could establish his family on the traditional basis of a good block of farmland, thus guaranteeing the family's subsistence in bad times, but still be close enough to the city for him and his sons to continue in business. For several generations most of the Tsangs lived, in fact, for most of the time near their urban businesses, and not in Tsang Tai Uk.

As to building his village with defensible walls and gates, this was a decision dictated by the troubled times in which Tsang Koon-man lived. It seems the Sha Tin area was always somewhat troubled by robbers and un-desirables as the main routes from the yamen at Kowloon City to Nantou, the then local administrative centre, passed through it. This route left Kowloon Walled City, and divided into two to cross the Lion Rock. One branch crossed mountains immediately south of Tsang Tai Uk, and went on to Tai Po, passing Tai Wai and crossing the passes at Tai Po Kau. The other branch crossed the mountains a little north of Tsang Tai Uk, and reached the coast at Yuen Chau Kok in Sha Tin . A ferry from Yuen Chau Kok carried traffic across Tolo Harbour to Chung Mei on Plover Cove. A further pass, through Ah Ma Wat, brought the road to Kuk Po from where a further ferry carried traffic to Sha Tau Kok. Piracy and banditry were common during the nineteenth century in this area, especially along major trading routes such as these, and the local people were wise to build secure villages.

Inter-village warfare was also common, and again led to a demand for villages with walls: Sha Tin , for instance, was at war with Cheung Sha Wan in the 1860s, while Tsang Tai Uk was under construction. The need for defence was, however, not due only to piracy and bandits but to a growing influx of newcomers from China in difficulties caused by a series of floods and famines, and hoping for a better life nearer the growing city of Hong Kong. These newcomers put a strain on already limited existing resources. Opium trading and kidnapping were also constant problems. Not surprisingly the village watch system operated in many villages in the New Territories until the 1960s, with a guard beating a gong or drum at half hourly intervals until dawn, when he sounded a reveille. Until 1962 the main entrance to Tsang Tai Uk was closed tight at 9 pm in accordance with this tradition of self-defence. The Tsang clan themselves say that their traditional self-defence practices were because, prior to the installation of the strong iron-ringed central gate, Tsang Koon-man's young son and daughter were kidnapped and taken into the interior, and only on payment of a ransom were the children safely returned.

Tsang Tai Uk was begun in 1848 and basically completed by 1865 or 1867, although some decorative features were still to be added as late as 1874. Seventeen or nineteen years is a long time, but, clearly, construction of a well-defended village able to fend off all the uncertainties of the period was no small undertaking. The design of Tsang Tai Uk generally follows the traditions of fortified villages in Tsang Koon-man's Cheung Lok homeland, although with sufficient significant local New Territories features (for instance, the eaves paintings, carved eaves boards, etc.) to make it likely that local masons did most of the actual building. The village is constructed from granite, solid timber, and locally made solid grey brick from Kak Tin, set in lime mortar.

The site of Tsang Tai Uk was low-lying and swampy, with a steep hill rising up immediately behind. Tsang Koon-man therefore started construction by building a large square platform, raised up a few feet from the swampy land, on which the village could safely be built. The village was built in two main phases. The earlier part consists of the ranges built around the Centre Court and the two Side Courts. This early part of the village is marked by four corner blocks which are still clearly discernible on the plan. Across the centre of this first phase building is the ritual heart of the village: the Entrance Hall, Clan Meeting Hall and Ancestral Hall, with the two parts of the Centre Court on either side of the Clan Meeting Hall. Tiny slip rooms, also originally used communally, open off both sides of the two parts of the Centre Court. The residential units in this first phase construction are small, and open off a maze of narrow passages and small inter-connecting courts. Much of this part of the village is rather dark.

At some date the outer ranges were added to this earlier core, forming the Front Court, East Court and West Court. The construction of these new ranges was butted onto the older core. The entrances to the older core have kept the locking bars and heavy doors which they had been given when they formed the outer defences of the village. Blocked gunposts can still be seen in the original corner blocks.

In the second phase ranges it is noticeable that the courtyards were built to a far more spacious plan than those in the earlier phase, making this section of the village far more light and airy. The residential units in this part of the village were also far larger, most of them with several rooms around a tiny private courtyard. While some of these units are now sub-divided, many of the tiny private courtyards and the original residential buildings survive.

We know from Tsang Koon-man's descendants that the ancestral hall and two small dwellings on either side were the first to be built. These were quarters for Tsang Koon-man himself, his wife, five of their six sons and their four daughters. The other accommodation was added as required as the family matured and expanded, and then more to cover hoped-for future growth. On completion there were far more residential units than were required by the Tsang family at the time. Some of the surplus units were, in fact, used to house a distillery, and a small weaving factory run by the Tsangs in the 1920s and 1930s. Tsang Koon-man called his village Shan Ha Wai ("The Defended Mansion by the Mountain"), but outsiders called it Tsang Tai Uk ("The Big House of the Tsangs") which is the commonly used name today.

Originally the front of the village faced a pond with lotus, and the entrance was by a causeway, over the low-lying fields, but both pond and causeway have long since disappeared. The tenets of fung shui were observed as far as could be: Tsang Koon-man himself attributed his wealth to careful observance of fung shui requirements. However, Tsang Tai Uk was founded several centuries after the other villages of the area, so the better fung shui sites were already occupied. There is a steep and well-wooded hill behind the village and the lotus pond provided water in front. The village faces north-west, in the optimum local fung shui direction. However, the fung shui on the western side was poor, and the clan planted a thick plantation of trees along this side to compensate: when the Lion Rock Tunnel road was built, this plantation was carefully replaced along the Tsang Tai Uk side of the road.

The village is rectangular (450 by 150 feet), and has several rows of dwellings, most (except the central Ancestral Hall block) being two storeys high. It has three entrances through the northern wall, all of which lead in to the long main Front Court around which village life revolves. Imposing as these entrances are, with their iron-ring and sheet-iron gates, a charming domestic note is struck as small holes have been made to facilitate feline nocturnal activity. Five entrances lead off this main courtyard, the central one to the Ancestral Hall and Meeting Hall, the others to the residential side courtyards. Over the outer entrances, Tsang Koon-man placed inscriptions outlining poignantly his hopes and aims in building the village: "A residence for endless generations", "where felicity summons innumerable blessings", "with riches and security", "with honour and glory", including a play on the name Koon-man ("endless and innumerable"). The calligraphy for these inscriptions was that of the then military commander at Kowloon City. The main, central, entrances, both that leading into the centre of the main courtyard, and that leading directly from the main courtyard to the Ancestral Hall complex, define the axis of ceremonial entry and form the main spine of the design.

Within the walls the dominant structure is the Ancestral Hall complex in the centre of the village. Opposite the central outer gate is an imposing entrance with high double-leaved doors under decorated and over-hanging eaves, leading via the Entrance Hall, to the Clan Meeting Hall. Here the elders met and adjudicated disputes and debated village problems. On occasions, at the end of the war,

TSANG TAI UK, CLAN MEETING HALL   RICHARD ABRAHALL

TSANG TAI UK, PORTRAITS OF VILLAGE FOUNDER AND HIS WIFE RICHARD ABRAHALL

At the centre of Tsang Tai Uk is the Ancestral Hall and clan Meeting Hall. In the Meeting Hall is the fine carved congratulatory screen presented to Tsang Koon-man on his 71st birthday, and portraits of Tsang Koon-man and his wife. Inside the Ancestral Hall the decorated lanterns hung every New Year to give thanks for the birth of new sons into the clan can be seen, to one side of the ancestral altar, which is marked with particularly fine carved woodwork.

TSANG TAI UK, ANCESTRAL ALTAR RICHARD ABRAHALL

TSANG TAI UK, ANCESTRAL HALL RICHARD ABRAHALL

the elders of the broader Sha Tin district met here. The furniture of this room has not survived, but a great carved screen, dated 1878, and covered with carved calligraphy, which stood behind the main seat when the elders met there, still stands.

This great screen was a gift to Tsang Koon-man. He bought himself an imperial degree sometime before his 71st birthday (by traditional Chinese reckoning) in 1878. He added an inscription to the central doorway of Tsang Tai Uk, "The Minister's Mansion" to celebrate this honour. He also held a big party to which all the high-ranking officials who had helped him achieve his honours were invited, and they gave him this screen as a gift. The screen lauds Tsang Koon-man's filial piety. Two other screens of a similar character and date survive in Hong Kong, at Kam Tin and Tai Hang. In accordance with the innocent flattery of such things, the screen adds ten years to Tsang Koon-man's age, suggesting he was then 81.

Behind the meeting room, across a small courtyard, is the Ancestral Hall. This boasts a magnificent carved altar-frame, extending from floor to ceiling. While in need of repair this altar-frame is one of the best pieces of traditional woodwork surviving in Hong Kong. It is similar in design and character to the slightly later altar-frame at Shan Tsui, near Sha Tau Kok. A few years ago, hidden high up on top of this Tsang Tai Uk altar-frame, was found a chest with the painted panels and other articles used in the ceremonies to placate the spirits when the ground for the village was first broken.

Whilst the massively high exterior walls of Tsang Tai Uk are of particular interest, the wok-yee ("frying pan handle") roof is also an outstanding feature. It is said that such a shaped roof indicates scholarship. Whether this refers to the fact that a distant family member gained 95th position in the Kui Yan Examinations in 1870 is questionable: more likely it refers to Tsang Koon-man's purchased honours. The metal tridents surmounting each roof are almost certainly there as protection against the intrusion of evil spirits, although Buddhists regard such tridents as insignia of power and authority.

In the main courtyard of Tsang Tai Uk are two wells, one at each end. Once they produced good quality drinking water, but today they are used only for laundry purposes as piped water was installed sixteen years ago.

The land in front of the village was previously used for farming and pigsheds, and worked by tenant farmers. Their now tumbledown dwellings can be seen to the north-east, just outside the walls of the village proper. They supplied the Tsang clan with food, having sufficient over to store or to market. The open ground immediately outside the entrances was used as a wo tong (rice-drying ground), but was also, it is said, used for fighting practice by the village guards. These tenants also staffed the Tsang's distillery enterprise.

Tsang Koon-man died in mid-summer 1888, at the age of 80. He was buried on the opposite side of Sha Tin Hoi, where his grave looked across the water to his "residence for endless generations". The grave had to be moved when the Kowloon-Canton Railway was built in 1912, and the grave was rebuilt behind the village, where it still stands. It was restored in 1993. When the new road behind the village was built in the 1980s, a new footpath was included to ensure continued access by his descendants to this grave.

Today, surrounded by high rise development, Tsang Tai Uk remains substantially unchanged in structure and layout, and reflects the continuing strength of tradition in the New Territories. It is still a fine traditional residence - despite the proliferation of protruding television aerials - as well as remaining the property of the Tsang clan. Many Tsangs have migrated and now only about 200 of the clansmen, mostly now in the sixth generation from Tsang Koon-man, remain in Hong Kong, and only a small percentage of these live in the village. As it has done over the decades, Tsang Tai Uk continues to offer a home to outsiders - presently about 300 people.

Rosemary Lee is a Council member of the RAS and Chairman of the Activities Committee. She was also a member of the Archaeological and Palaeontological Committee of the Antiquities Advisory Board, and Director of the Community Advisory Bureau.

TSANG TAI UK, ENTRANCE TO SIDE COURT   JANET STOTT

Access from the Front Court of Tsang Tai Uk to the Side Courts, and to the East and West Courts,
is through stone-framed doors and stone lined passages like these.

TSANG TAI UK, ENTRANCE TO SIDE COURT   RICHARD ABRAHALL

The Front Court at Tsang Tai Uk has fine, stone-lined wells at either end. Looking from it to the south, the view is still to the fung shui hill, but, to the north, the presence of the tower blocks of the adjacent estates witnesses to the village's position in the centre of the Sha Tin New Town.

TSANG TAI UK, FRONT COURT   JANET STOTT

TSANG TAI UK, ENTRANCE TO ANCESTRAL HALL
ANDY DOMERACKI

TSANG TAI UK, MAIN GATE   RICHARD STOTT

TSANG TAI UK, FRONT COURT AND WELL
RICHARD ABRAHALL

TSANG TAI UK, EXTERIOR   RICHARD ABRAHALL

TSANG TAI UK, EXTERIOR   RICHARD ABRAHALL

Tsang Tai Uk was built in phases over several decades, and the rear wall in particular shows where the various stages of building butt against each other. The other exterior walls show the clutter which tends to mark the perimeters of villages.

TSANG TAI UK, EXTERIOR   RICHARD ABRAHALL

TSANG TAI UK, EXTERIOR, REAR WALL
RICHARD ABRAHALL

TSANG TAI UK, SMALL ROOMS OFF THE CENTRE COURT   ANDY DOMERACKI

TRADITIONAL WEDDING, TSANG TAI UK, FRONT COURT
RICHARD ABRAHALL

TSANG TAI UK, CENTRE COURT RICHARD ABRAHALL

TSANG TAI UK, ENTRANCE TO CENTRE COURT RICHARD ABRAHALL

Plenty of people still live in Tsang Tai Uk, where elements of traditional weddings can still be seen, and where friends still gather to gossip on the steps of the entrance to the Central Court. Bamboo racks for washing are still to be found in the Front Court, and a tiny cat still uses the cat hole considerately left by the builders of the Main Gate, so the local cats could come and go when the great gates were shut and locked.

TSANG TAI UK, MAIN GATE   RICHARD ABRAHALL

TSANG TAI UK, FRONT COURT   JANET STOTT

TSANG TAI UK   TONY HEDLEY

TSANG TAI UK   RICHARD ABRAHALL

TSANG TAI UK, ENTRANCE TO CENTRE COURT   TONY HEDLEY

Villagers like to feel that they are secure against bandits and thieves. Heavy timber or even iron gates, lockable wooden sliding bars which fit into stout granite sockets, as at the entrance to the Centre Court, heavy plank doors with reinforcing bars - all are to be found in most villages, not just Tsang Tai Uk, although they are found there in abundance.

TSANG TAI UK, ENTRANCE TO CENTRE COURT   TONY HEDLEY

TSANG TAI UK, MAIN GATE   TONY HEDLEY

TSANG TAI UK   TONY HEDLEY

PHOTOGRAPHERS

Richard Abrahall, ARPS, has been teaching photography and economics at Island School since 1971. He is single-minded in his love for monochrome and spends hours locked away in the dark room trying to catch up with printing the backlog that results form his frequent excursions around the world. He gained his distinction from the Royal Photographic Society in 1992.

Kim Aplin, ARPS, read Fine Arts at university before joining the Police Force in Hong Kong in 1974. Some of his early experience with the RHKP was policing the New Territories and he has been fascinated by this area ever since, as is reflected in his work in both colour and monochrome. He gained his distinction form the Royal Photographic Society in 1994.

Andy Domeracki travels widely around Asia with his work as a marketing director, and usually finds time to use his camera in spare moments. He progressed from general photography to specialising in underwater photography, and has only recently extended his interest to incorporate black and white images, with considerable success.

Tony Hedley is Professor of Community Medicine at the University of Hong Kong. He is a collector of cameras and photographic memorabilia and has been photographing Asia for thirty years. A keen aviator, Tony has extended his photographic perspective to birdseye panoramas.

John Lambon is creative in many media. He works as an architect but enjoys painting and drawing, stage design and lighting, still photography and video in his spare time. Primarily a worker in colour, he has been mainly involved as the Graphic Adviser of this book, liaising with the RAS, f8 and the publisher.

Janet Stott, ARPS, is a court stenographer who finds time to travel widely, always taking her camera and binoculars. Her interests include patchwork and quilting and birdwatching and she has become an enthusiastic photographer over the past eight years. She gained her distinction from the Royal Photographic Society in 1994 and her black and white panel, based on photographs for this book, was used by the RPS for its workshops. She has been living in Hong Kong since 1983.

Richard Stott, LRPS, is an engineer by profession and an enthusiastic traveller, combining his passion for birdwatching (he is Chairman of the Hong Kong Birdwatching Society) with photography. He is a committed dark room worker and gained his distinction from the Royal Photographic Society in 1993. He has been living in Hong Kong since 1981.

GLOSSARY

Placenames within Hong Kong are transliterated in the text as in the *Hong Kong Gazetteer of Placenames* (1961), and the Chinese characters for these placenames are given below. Placenames in China are transliterated in *pinyin:* Chinese characters for placenames below provincial level are given below. Other words are transliterated into either *pinyin* or Cantonese, with Chinese characters given below. Most personal names are transliterated into Cantonese.

A Ma Wat 亞媽笏
Au Ha 凹下
Changle 長樂
Chaozhou 潮州
Chau 鄒
Chau Hing-wah 鄒興華
Chek Lap Kok 赤鱲角
Cheung 張
Cheung Chau 長洲
Cheung Sha Wan 長沙灣
Cheung Shan Kwu Tsz 長山古寺
Cheung Uk 張屋
Chik Chuen Wai 積存圍
Ching Ming 清明
Ching Shu Hin 清暑軒
Chue Tseuk 赤雀
Chung 鍾
Chung Mei 涌尾
Chung Yeung 重陽
Dabu 大埔
Dongguan 東莞
Guo Ziyi 郭子儀
Fanling (Wai) 粉嶺 (圍)
Fu 釜
Fui Shing 魁星
Fung Shui 風水
Fung Yuen 鳳園
Ha Fu 下夫
Ha Hang 下坑
Hakka 客家
Hak Lung 黑龍
Han 漢
Hang Ha Po 坑下莆
Hang Heung 行鄉
Hang Mei 坑尾
Hang Tau 坑頭
Ha Tsuen 廈村
Ha Wo Hang 下禾坑
Hau 侯
Hei 氣
Ho 何
Ho Chung 蠔涌
Hok Tau (Wai) 鶴藪 (圍)
Ho Lek Pui 河瀝背
Ho Nam-han 何南漢
Ho Sheung Heung 河上鄉
Hung Fa Tsai 紅花仔
Hung Leng 孔嶺
Hung Leng Sze Yeuk 孔嶺四約
Hung Shing 洪聖
Hung Shui Kiu 紅水橋
Jiayingzhou 嘉應州
Kaito 街渡
Kaiping 開平
Kai Yik Kok 雞翼角
Kak Tin 隔田
Kan 簡
Kang Fu 耕夫
Kan Tau 簡頭
Kam Tin 錦田

Kam Tsin 金錢
Kat Hing Wai 吉慶圍
Keng Hau 逕口
Keung Shan 羗山
Kim Hau 鉗口
Kiu-lam 喬林
Kong Ha 崗下
Ko Po 高莆
Koxinga 國姓爺
Kui Yan 舉人
Kuk Po 谷埔
Kwai Tau Leng 龜頭嶺
Kwan Din 坤甸
Kwan Tei 軍地
Kwok 郭
Kwun Yam 觀音
Lam 林
Lantau 大嶼山
Lau Fau Shan 流浮山
Lau Shui Heung 流水响
Lee (see Lei)
Lei 李
Lei Ngong-ying 李昂英
Lei Tsz-ching 李子禎
Lei Wai-yan 李維仁
Lei Uk 李屋
Leng Pei (or Ling Pei) 嶺皮
Li 里
Li Wanzong 李萬宗
Ling Tsai 嶺仔
Lin Au 蓮澳
Little Hong Kong 香港圍
Liu 廖
Lo Hsun 盧循
Loi Tung 萊洞
Longan 龍眼
Lo Wai 老圍
Luk Yeuk 六約
Lung Kwu Tan 龍鼓灘
Lung Yeuk Tau 龍躍頭
Nai Wai 泥圍
Nam Fung 南風
Nam Mo Lo 喃嘸佬
Nautou 南頭
Nantoushan 南頭山
Nga Tsin Wai 衙前圍
Ngau Kwu Long 牛牯塱
Ngong Wo 昂窩
Ninghua 寧化
Pak Fu 白虎
Pak Hok Lam 白鶴林
Pak Mong 白芒
Pak Tam Chung 北潭涌
Pang 彭
Pat Heung 八鄉
Pat Sin 八仙
Ping Kong 丙崗
Ping Shan 屏山
Ping Shan Chai 平山寨

Ping Yeung 坪洋
Po Tak 寶德
Punti 本地
Qu Lie 曲烈
Sai Kung 西貢
Sai Man 細民
Sam Li 三利
Sam Li Quarry 三利石塘
Sam Tung Uk 三棟屋
San Tong Po 新塘莆
San Tin 新田
San Uk Ha 新屋下
San Uk Tsai 新屋仔
San Wai 新圍
Sha Kong Miu 沙江廟
Sha Lo Tung 沙螺洞
Sham 沈
Shan Ha Wai 山廈圍
Shan Shek Wan 礐石灣
Shanghang 上坑
Shap Yeuk 十約
Shat 煞
Sha Tau Kok 沙頭角
Sha Tin 沙田
Sha Tin Kau Yeuk 沙田九約
Sha Tin Hoi 沙田海
Shao Kang 少康
Shau Kei Wan 筲箕灣
Shek Chung Au 石涌凹
Shek Kiu Tau 石橋頭
Shek Pik 石壁
Shenzhen 深圳
Sheung Cheung Wai 上璋圍
Sheung Ling Pei 上嶺皮
Sheung Shui 上水
Sheung Wo Hang 上禾坑
Sheung Yiu 上窰
Shing Hin Kung 聖軒公
Shing Mun 城門
Shut Hing 述卿
Songyuan 松源
Ta Ho Tun 打蠔墩
Ta Kwu Leng 打鼓嶺
Tai Hang 太坑
Tai Ho 大蠔
Tai Hong Wai 泰康圍
Tai Long 大朗
Tai Mong Tsai 大網仔
Tai O 大澳
Tai Po 大埔
Tai Po Kau 大埔滘
Tai Po Mei 大埔尾
Tai Po Tau 大埔頭
Taishan 泰山
Tai Shan 泰山
Tai Wai 大圍
Tai Wan 大環
Tan 蛋
Tan Chuk Hang 丹竹坑
Tang 鄧

Tang Fung-shun 鄧馮遜
Tang Kai-cheung 鄧啟昌
Tang Kai-ching 鄧啟徵
Tang Kai-yuen 鄧啟元
Tang Kun-ting 鄧冠廷
Tang Sai-chiu 鄧世昭
Tang Sai-yin 鄧世賢
Tang Sung-yi 鄧崇義
Tang Yung-keng 鄧蓉鏡
Tan Shan 丹山
Tat Tak 達德
Ta Tsiu 打醮
Tau 斗
Tau Chung 斗種
Tin Hau 天后
Tin Sam 田心
Tolo Harbour 吐路海
Tsang 曾
Tsang Koon-man 曾貫萬
Tsang Sam-li 曾三利
Tsang Tai Uk 曾大屋
Tsat Yeuk 七約
Tseng Mau 鄑巫
Tsing Lung 青龍
Tsing Yi 青衣
Tso Wo Hang 早禾坑
Tsui Shing Lau 聚星樓
Tsun Sz 進士
Tuen Mun 屯門
Tuen Ng 端午
Tung Chung 東涌
Tung Lung 東龍
Wai 圍
Wai Ha 圍下
Wai Noi 圍內
Wangbeiling 黃貝嶺
Wang Hang 橫坑
Wing Lung Wai 永隆圍
Wok Yee 鑊耳
Wong 黃
Wong Chuk Shan 黃竹山
Wong Chuk Wan 黃竹灣
Wong Yi Chau 黃宜洲
Yamen 衙門
Yang 陽
Yao 猺
Yau Yue Wan 魷魚灣
Yeuk 約
Yeuk Hoi 若虛
Yeung Hau Wong 楊侯王
Yin 陰
Yip 葉
Yuen Chau Kok 圓洲角
Yuen Long 元朗
Yu Kiu 愈喬
Yu Sing 愈聖
Xinhui 新會